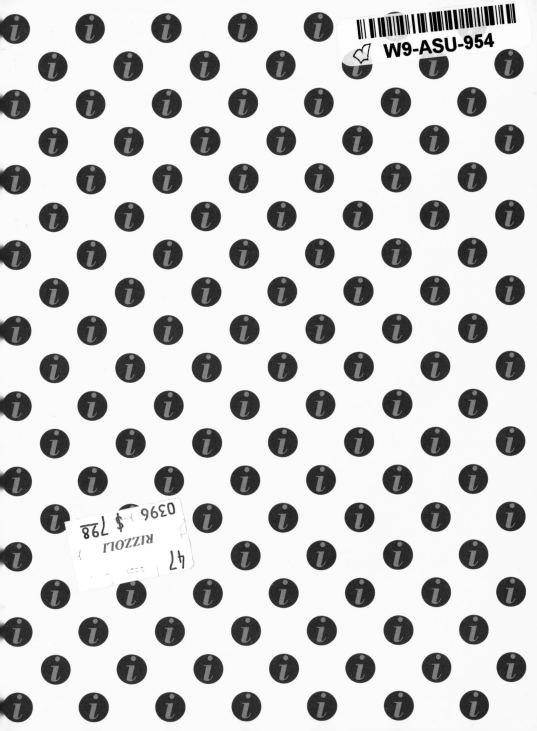

IDENTIFYING

TEDDY BEARS

The new compact study guide and identifier

I D E N T I F Y I N G

TEDDY BEARS

The new compact study guide and identifier

Margaret and Gerry Grey

CHARTWELL
BOOKS, INC.

A QUINTET BOOK

Published by Chartwell Books
A Division of Book Sales, Inc.
114 Northfield Avenue
Edison, New Jersey 08837

ISBN 0-7858-0574-5

This book was designed and produced by
Quintet Publishing Limited
6 Blundell Street
London N7 9BH

Creative Director: Richard Dewing
Designer: James Lawrence
Project Editor: Anna Briffa
Editor: Jane Donovan
Photographers: Nick Bailey and Jeremy Thomas

Typeset in Great Britain by
Central Southern Typesetters, Eastbourne
Manufactured in China by
Regent Publishing Services Ltd
Printed in China by
Leefung-Asco Printers Ltd

CONTENTS

INTRODUCTION

It is only about 15 years since a talented but obscure actor, Peter Bull, whose face was instantly recognizable but whose name is hardly ever remembered, first alerted people to the joys of collecting teddy bears by talking with such enthusiasm about them on British and American television. At the time it was unusual to know precisely what an arctophile is – a person who loves teddy bears – let alone be a collector of teddy bears.

The USA, which was and still is the world's leading teddy bear nation, provided the necessary driving force for this new phenomenon to continue into the 1980s, but several years passed before it spread to other parts of the world. Teddy bear collecting is now, however, one of the most popular collecting interests worldwide. Prices for all bears have escalated in recent years, culminating in the record-breaking sale at auction (for £55,000/$86,000) of "Happy" in 1989. All collectors naturally live in hope that one day they will find their own "Happy", but teddy bear collecting is so much more than good investment.

Over the years, many authors have tried to analyse precisely what the appeal of a teddy bear is. Although challenging, this is quite unnecessary and probably an impossible task. The word "Happy" seems to epitomize the sheer beauty and character we all seek in our teddy bears – gaze into those great big eyes and your heart just melts! It is precisely this reaction that should be experienced with any bear – love and appreciation – rather than thinking about its potential as an investment. Collect only what appeals to you and not just what you think might be valuable and that way you will not be disappointed. In fact for the majority of people the most "precious" bear, regardless of financial investment, in their collection will be the first bear they ever owned, loved and cherished since childhood.

ABOVE "Happy" – a 1926 Steiff – is seen here in her role as mascot of the "Teddies of the World '93" convention.

FROM TOY BEAR TO TEDDY BEAR (1903–18)

The true origins of the teddy bear probably go back to the Middle Ages when people were fascinated by real wild bears. Unfortunately, these poor tortured beasts were used throughout Europe purely for entertainment – as dancing bears. Hundreds of years later the Victorians began the trend for real bears to be kept in zoos – again for the entertainment of the masses.

At the end of the 19th century Stuttgart Zoo in Germany was frequently visited by a young toy designer from Giengen-en-Brenz named Richard Steiff, a nephew of the renowned toy producer Margarete Steiff. He was interested in all animals but bears particularly intrigued him. Life-like bears had been made by Steiff for some five or six years previously but they were based on fully grown bears, and were therefore difficult to play with. Richard sketched little bear cubs and it was these that influenced Steiff's prototype of the first toy bear late in 1902.

This toy bear was part of a small range of movable (*beweglich*) animals employing disc joints (*angeschiebt*) which formed part of a shipment of toys to New York around the middle of February 1903. Its general shape and appearance closely resembled a real bear with a long shaven snout, very long arms, stout body, big feet and the quite distinctive back hump.

It is important to consider the period of time required for designing and then producing this new range.

Clifford Berryman's famous cartoon of President Theodore (Teddy) Roosevelt appeared in the *Washington Post* on November 16, 1902. Communications in those days were so limited that we doubt that this cartoon could have had any influence on Richard Steiff, as is often suggested.

However, it is thought, though not substantiated, that the cartoon was responsible for Russian immigrants Morris and Rose Michtom, who were novelty and stationery storekeepers of Brooklyn, New York, creating the first toy bears made in America. Subsequently – and presumably rather later in 1903 – the Michtoms' toy bears were bought by a large wholesale company, Butler Bros., and distributed throughout the USA.

It would take a considerable time to design, develop and then make a range of quality prototype toys for export to the USA. Commonsense therefore suggests that Steiff's own toy bear was in fact the world's first! However, both Steiff and the Michtoms, who set up The Ideal Novelty and Toy Co., can justly claim they were pioneers of the original teddy bear. The dramatic last-minute purchase of 3,000 of Steiff's bears at the Leipzig Toy Fair in March 1903 by Herman Berg of Geo Borgfeldt, the world-famous

American toy importers, when everyone else had ignored them, was incredibly fortuitous.

While Steiff's bear closely resembles a real bear, the Ideal version is much more similar to Berryman's own cartoon bear cub and, therefore, rather more like the teddy bear we know. Clifford Berryman continued to draw many cartoons associated with President Roosevelt, and, eventually, these were probably the greatest single influence in coining the term "teddy bear" that we now use.

During those early years both firms developed their ranges, but it was not very long before Steiff's greater experience of toy design and production, coupled with Richard's imaginative ideas for bears of such variety and sheer quality, enabled them to become the world's premier manufacturer. Conversely, Ideal's bears appear to have hardly changed from their first design.

Steiff's first bear in 1903 was referred to as the 55PB, followed by the 35PB in early 1904. Both used disc joints held together by a strong string cord. Unfortunately, these were found to be rather impractical, and broke so easily that Steiff changed briefly to using double wires, but this proved to be far too dangerous. This led quickly to the development of the

– TEDDY DISTRIBUTORS IN THE USA –

Influential importers/wholesalers who distributed teddy bears throughout the USA at that time are worth mentioning. Many of them persuaded manufacturers to make and supply bears, some of which they may have marketed under their own names.

GEO BORGFELDT & COMPANY was the greatest of all these firms and was responsible for that first eventful purchase of 3,000 teddy bears from Steiff at the Leipzig Spring Toy Fair in 1903. Had they not done this, we might never have had a teddy bear craze at all! Borgfeldt's influence on the toy industry was legendary.

BUTLER BROS. took over the marketing and distribution of the early Ideal Toy and Novelty Co teddy bears. They also distributed a range of Steiff bears from about 1908 onwards.

STROBEL & WILKEN CO were notable as distributors for BMC.

E.L. HORSMAN & COMPANY were distributors for Hecla and Aetna bears. It was Horsman & Co who first used the name "teddy" in an advertisement in the American trade magazine *Playthings* in December 1906.

– TEDDY DISTRIBUTORS IN THE UK –

During these early formative years there were two major importers and distributors in the UK. **Josef Eisenmann**, or "Jo" as he was popularly known, was acknowledged as the "King of the Toy Trade" in the UK. Eisenmann & Co were importers and distributors of toys, particularly those from Germany, but it was Jo who suggested to J. K. Farnell that they should make teddy bears to combat the influx of Steiff products. Jo was also the father-in-law of Leon Rees, who eventually in 1920 collaborated with Harry G. Stone to take over the manufacture of the famous "Chiltern" range.

From 1899 until the outbreak of World War I in 1914, **Herbert E. Hughes** was the sole importer of Steiff products to the UK. In the Ciesliks' book, *Button in the Ear*, they report the close relationship that existed between Otto Steiff and Herbert. Hughes's major clients in Britain were Harrods, Hamleys, Gamages and Josef Eisenmann himself. Because of this association Herbert would almost certainly have had a detailed knowledge of Steiff and the German industry. In 1908 he was responsible for an order of *40,000* Steiff bears just for the UK! Hughes ceased his involvement with Steiff at the outbreak of World War I.

famous rod bears where a metal rod was passed through the upper body of the bear attaching the arms, with a vertical T-rod connecting and supporting the head, and another rod attaching the legs. The head was stuffed from the top and to facilitate this, a horizontal seam from ear to ear was provided. This bear is usually referred to as the 28PB.

Unfortunately, this bear was rather awkward in its movement and its large rotund body really did not have sufficient child appeal. After only a year (1905), this led to the production of the *Barle* (meaning someone dear) range of PAB bears. Their great virtue was that they were softer, filled with a mixture of excelsior and kapok, thus making them far more cuddly than their predecessors, and more appealing to children!

This was a great breakthrough and the turning point for Steiff. The PAB35 is assumed to have been the first of a range that came in seven sizes from 17 cm/6½ in up to 80 cm/32 in, but because the bear was lighter in weight and the articulated body was held together by a conventional double disc joint and metal pin, it had a more acceptable and reliable movement. (Incidentally, to establish the size of this range of bears always measure in the *seated* position.)

ABOVE The 1908 cover of The Sketch *picturing a teddy bear at the Chicago rally to elect President Taft. The caption is "Teddy Bear in Politics: the Cause of the Rumpus".*

Around the same time Richard Steiff also produced his now famous prototype – a small grey bear referred to as model 5322 (33 cm / 13 in). Steiff's archives suggest that only two of these were made and perhaps a few others as samples. This must be one of the rarest and possibly the most valuable bears on earth. An example can be found in the Steiff Museum.

Franz Steiff, another of Margarete's nephews, had the previous year decided to implement a trademark standard by introducing the metal button in the ear "Knopf im Ohr", a symbol used ever since. Initially, the elephant button was used, followed later that year (1904) by a plain blank button (not to be confused with the blank blue button used briefly between 1948 and 1950), superseded in May 1905 by an inscribed STEIFF button when Steiff finally had their unique trademark confirmed.

There is some controversy over the exact dating of the buttons – most authorities now suggest the order we give but others believe the blank button came first. Both may have been used simultaneously, although we suspect the elephant button was possibly the first because this happened to be Steiff's logo at the time. Logic, however, suggests the blank button might have been used initially simply because it was easier and more convenient to produce. In the USA in 1906, the name "Teddy" was adopted and the ubiquitous "teddy bear" was officially christened.

Meanwhile, in the USA teddy bear manufacturers were emerging (mainly around New York), who probably drew on the experience and knowledge of emigrant toy workers flocking there from Europe. Despite innumerable claims by American manufacturers that their bears compared in quality to those from Steiff, they emphatically did not! One thing, however, we have to thank those early American firms for was their inventiveness – bears that whistled, musical bears, and of course the redoubtable bright-eyed teddy, which had eyes illuminated by an inbuilt battery – were but a few of the intriguing new features they gave to teddy bears. It was this that influenced manufacturers in other countries.

Teddy bear manufacture did not begin in the UK until 1908 when J. K. Farnell began production. Unfortunately the British public were not immediately enthralled by their bears and Farnells were forced to export almost their entire stock to the USA, South Africa and even Germany!

The world trade in teddy bears reached its peak in 1907 when Steiff's production alone was a little under 1,000,000 teddy bears. Some companies that sprang up simply produced imitations of Steiff bears but there were innovators such as Gebrüder Bing. They were responsible for developing the clockwork mechanism for bears (1908–10) used for roller-skating bears, acro or tumbling bears and even bears pushing balls. The boom was followed almost immediately by a slump during which several manufacturers in Germany and the USA ceased trading overnight. Some new companies did appear such as Schuco (Schreyer and Co) and Gebrüder Hermann Kg. With the outbreak of war in 1914, German goods were prohibited in the UK and the instant demise of the competition persuaded several British companies to start teddy bear production. Many companies began by copying Steiff products, but it was not long before they started producing original designs for quality bears.

BEARS BETWEEN THE WARS (1919–39)

Immediately following World War I, a period of instability afflicted world markets and many of the firms who had previously been producing teddy bears suddenly found themselves in financial trouble and had to cease trading.

Steiff, by then a well-established and world-leading manufacturer, experienced tremendous difficulty attempting to re-establish the pre-eminence they had enjoyed during the decade leading up to the war, and their struggle was intensified due mainly to a backlash of resentment in Britain and America. Broadly speaking, the German toy industry had no choice but to adopt lower prices during these inflationary times, and many organizations with a vested interest such as The British Toy Federation rather disparagingly referred to "cheap" German toys which the public should avoid!

The Japanese toy industry, in concert with many of their other industries at the time, were then beginning to expand and their cheaper exports were becoming a threat to all. Elsewhere – France and Australia in particular – manufacturers began producing for their domestic markets.

The USA was the world's largest market for toys but their own domestic teddy bear manufacturing base was by now much depleted. Unfortunately, very few

– COLLECTORS' NOTES 1919–39 –

Due to the large number of teddy bear manufacturers all over the world at this time, you have a good chance of finding high-quality teddy bears from this era. However, many of the earlier bears, those from the 1920s for example, made by the more famous quality producers will be expensive.

– COMMONWEALTH TOY AND NOVELTY COMPANY (1934) –

This American company introduced the rather unusual "Feed me" bear. The teddy could be fed by pulling a cord at the back of his head so that his mouth would open to swallow food. The food could be retrieved by unzipping the bear. Although not very attractive, these bears are novel and certainly worth looking for.

– GUND INC (1906) –

For a major company, it is quite surprising to find there are few examples of teddy bears made during these early years. So far, few quality bears from this era have ever been properly identified, so these might be quite a find.

– LOUIS GOLDBERG (1935) –

This British company offered the "cheapest grade of soft toys that have ever been produced in England" – brave words. The result was a fairly nondescript bear which will be hard to identify due to the millions of similar bears at the time. Look for square shoulders, close-fitting legs, very pointed tapering arms, and a chest tag inscribed "Hygienic Toys" with the word "Teddy" centrally located.

– EDUARD CRAMER (1930) –

These German bears from the early 1930s were clearly influenced by Steiff's "Teddy Baby" line and have similar features. A musical walking bear was based on the Steiff's "Clown" line with the same frosted mohair. One of the main features of these bears was the completely shaven snout. The bears had inset eyes, button-style noses, and partially open mouths, exposing soft pink felt tongues. The latter is unmistakably Cramer's most distinguishing feature, although the company also made closed-mouth bears.

of the new American companies of the time managed to make much of a name for themselves, with the possible exception of Knickerbocker, as consumers preferred the imported bears. Even the well-established firms, such as Ideal and Gund, seemed to lack the ability to produce appealing teddy bears.

The UK, on the other hand, had rather successfully managed to retain almost all of its quality soft toy manufacturing base and it was these companies who were subsequently able to prove their potential for producing original ideas. During the next two decades several British companies were to establish themselves as equal to any. The most notable newcomer in the UK was Merrythought, established in 1930.

A popular feature of British bears at the time was the new style of soft-filled bears; the Teddy Toy Company produced "Softanlite", followed by W. J. Terry with "Ahsolight". Chad Valley had the "Aerolite" range and many other manufacturers followed. There was also keen competition to present bears as hygienic toys and the Institute of Hygiene mark of approval

was highly coveted. In 1929, just before the Great Depression, the Teddy Toy Company introduced the new and cheaper art silk plush instead of mohair, while Chiltern followed shortly afterwards with their "Silky" teddy and Farnell's "Silkalite" range.

In Germany manufacturing had recommenced after World War I but Steiff were finding things difficult. For some years they had persisted with their old designs, until around 1925 when Richard Steiff wrote from the USA that Steiff bears "appear colourless, sober and insipid". These harsh words seemed just the jolt the company needed and the result was a new generation of imaginative and original designs. It was at this time that "Happy" was produced, though it seems that very few bears of this type were made.

The firm Schreyer and Co, better known as Schuco, began this era with a unique bear design – the "Yes-No" series that had a mechanical linkage device concealed within the tail enabling the head to move up or down (nodding or shaking its head).

The depression (1929–32) had severely weakened the foundations of virtually all teddy bear manufacturers and with the threat of another war, it is not surprising that the genre of bears made during the late 1930s lacked the variety of the previous 30 years.

ABOVE A British postcard from c. 1936 showing HRH the Duchess of York, the future Queen Mother, holding a wonderful English bear from the era, probably by J. K. Farnell.

POSTWAR RECOVERY (1946–60)

Ravaged by the two world wars, disrupted by serious economic problems, many of the world's teddy bear manufacturers ceased to exist. A difficult time was in store for all the acknowledged quality toy manufacturers as they tried to pick up the pieces and re-establish themselves. They could not possibly foresee that within three decades the world would drastically change beyond all recognition as the new technological age and throw-away society evolved. No longer were children encouraged to nurture their beloved favourite toy – toys soon became plentiful and children less considerate and far more demanding for the very latest TV toy! Cheap goods were the prerequisite of the post-war baby boom.

It is surprising, therefore, that the most successful were the quality manu-

ABOVE An unusual bear made by Lefray Ltd in the mid 1950s (height 53 cm/21 in). It is made to stand with very short fixed legs, but the head and arms are articulated. The ears are lined with brown velvet and the nostrils are red in colour.

facturers such as Steiff, Schuco, Hermann, Chiltern and Chad Valley. Sadly, their success was short-lived as the multi-national conglomerate toy companies – usually American – just swallowed up all and sundry as they sought to control mass markets. No company was safe and all felt the threat of these big boys, as well as the threat of the continued rise of Japan as a major toy-producing nation.

To compound the problems for teddy bear manufacturers, the Americans introduced new stringent safety regulations in the late 1950s and these were soon to spread to other countries.

The teddy bears which followed from the mid-1950s right through to the 1970s were certainly soft and cuddly, made to conform to international safety standards, and above all, cheap.

ABOVE This wonderful Chad Valley teddy c. 1950 is bidding farewell to an old friend – a Steiff c. 1905.

– COLLECTORS' NOTES 1946–60 –

Unfortunately for collectors, the new safety rules so profoundly affected and restricted the design and manufacture of teddy bears that after about 1960 they are generally lacking in character and appeal.

– CHARACTER NOVELTY CO. –

The bears produced by this American company after the war and in the 1950s used the unusual technique of black button eyes applied to a white felt backing. This firm used a printed label bearing the name "Character" which was sewn into the left ear.

– PEDIGREE SOFT TOYS LTD. (1937) –

This was the name of a line of stuffed toys produced under the banner of Lines Brothers from 1937. The quality varied from good to poor, but the distinctive feature was a nose placed high on the face with a long lip extending down to the mouth. The bears were made in London until 1955 when production was transferred to Northern Ireland.

– W.T. CO. –

A soft-bodied wind-up teddy was produced in 1951 that danced and walked, and another magic eye (battery-operated) bear. These bears also had triangular foot pads.

– HERMANN-SPIELWAREN GMBH (1920) –

The Hermann-Spielwaren company was formerly known as Max Hermann & Sohn with premises in Sonneberg. In 1947, Max Hermann changed the name of the firm to Hermann & Co Kg, which had premises in both Sonneberg and Coburg. In 1953, Max moved the whole firm from Sonneberg to Coburg, where it has remained ever since. There were not, therefore, two different Hermann firms! Look for the early two-tone frosted mohair bear model 73. The firm used a green triangular pressed metal tag with a walking bear and a dog as its trademark.

– FETCHER –

Immediately after World War II, this firm began manufacturing in Graz, Austria, and an open-mouthed bear was a prominent feature of their line. Easily distinguishable by their very large round heads, inset snouts, and very large ears which usually had different coloured lined inner ears placed at the top of the heads. The Fetcher label was sewn to the outside of the bear's right ear. Quite often, red-coloured eyes were used.

– S. OPPENHEIMER LTD. –

This German company produced teddy bears under the trademark "EMU" in 1950, distinguished by their triangular footpads.

THE AGE OF SPECIAL EDITION BEARS

After nearly two decades – the 1960s and 1970s – when very few bears of serious interest to collectors were produced, 1980 marked the start of a new and exciting era. It was Margarete Steiff GmbH which was again to dominate, reaffirming its position as the leading manufacturer of quality soft toys and teddy bears.

Spurred on by the need for a fresh approach to fight off the threat of cheap imports, Steiff introduced a special edition teddy bear in 1980 to commemorate the 100th anniversary of the company. Its success enabled the firm to implement state of the art production methods to reproduce the originals kept in the Steiff museum, which had also opened that year, as faithfully as possible, modern materials permitting.

ABOVE This is a full set of the delightful 1909 replicas issued by Steiff between 1983 and 1988. The smaller and larger bears were issued only to the USA.

ABOVE One of the best contemporary Steiffs – the first of the British Collector's series is a 1989 replica of a 1907 bear (height 61cm/24 in).

Steiff regularly made exclusive limited editions for major department stores worldwide and also produced editions for Disney World and Disneyland Conventions held annually in the U.S.

Many, but by no means all, of the Steiff replica bears have appreciated in value, some substantially, which may be an inducement to some collectors. So many special limited edition bears have been issued that a reference chart of those produced by Steiff until 1993 is given on pages 55–62. Only limited editions carrying white tags have been included. Although some absolutely wonderful yellow-tag (standard production) bears were produced, it is impossible to list them, too.

Many of the yellow tags are highly collectible, and some can be rather expensive; perhaps the most desirable are the early "Mr. Cinnamon" bears made in three sizes and several ranges of the "Margaret Strong" bears produced in the mid-1980s.

– COLLECTOR'S NOTES
DEANS RAG BOOK CO LTD (1915)
(NOW THE DEANS COMPANY (1903) –

This is another British company which realized the importance of the collectors' market, when in 1981 they produced bears for the USA based on Norman Rockwell drawings. They have continued to manufacture collectible bears and in the past few years their range has substantially improved.

– LITTLE FOLK (1980) –

From the outset in 1980 Little Folk realized there was greater potential in the USA where most of their bears were exported. Their very early designs used mohair but this meant the bears were probably too expensive and cheaper acrylic plush was successfully introduced *circa* 1982. This same range is produced today and much in demand.

A 2,000 limited edition bear Sebastian (1987) and 500 No Jonathon's (1900) have also been produced with collectors in mind. We have a special place in our hearts for Little Folk bears because these were the first contemporary bears we ever sold.

– MERRYTHOUGHT LTD (1930) –

In 1982 Merrythought decided to introduce a range of limited edition bears, usually based on their old designs, for the USA market. Recently several new designs have been added, including those inspired by John Axe (author of *The Magic of Merrythought*) and others based on the drawings of the English illustrator, Prue Theobalds.

– HOUSE OF NISBET (1978) –

Of all the contemporary manufacturers, the House of Nisbet under the leadership of Jack Wilson were probably the most adventurous. He cultivated an extremely fruitful business relationship with the amazing Peter Bull, resulting in the introduction of the "Bully Bear" range, and the delightful edition of 12 "Zodiac" bears, based on a book by Pauline McMillan and Peter Bull. It was a very great loss to the teddy bear world when Jack decided to retire in 1989 and the House of Nisbet was taken over by Dakin.

"Delicatessen" ("Aloysius"), another of Peter Bull's bears, is without equal and incidentally was directly responsible for the introduction of distressed mohair which artists have since found so helpful.

The "Nisbet Celebrity" collection was an inspired move by the astute Jack who had been quick to realize that there were other "celebrities" in the rapidly expanding Teddy Bear collecting fraternity. In 1987 he invited well-known people to have a bear made in their name or asked artists to design a special bear.

TEDDY BEAR IDENTIFIER

BRUIN BEAR

FIRST KNOWN YEAR OF PRODUCTION *c.* **1907/8**
MANUFACTURER **Bruin Manufacturing Company**
COUNTRY OF ORIGIN **USA** HEIGHT **32 cm (12½in)**

The Bruin Manufacturing Company was established in1907, but had folded by 1909. Many American companies failed after only a few years and this makes their bears even more desirable and sought after.

Look for the woven black label with BMC inscribed in gold letters and fixed centrally across the breadth of the right foot.

The distinguishing features of Bruin Bears are their wide-apart ears with rather triangular shaped heads, which adds to their appeal.

If you are lucky enough to own one of these bears, or if you spot one in an auction or sale room, then they are highly valuable and are likely to increase in value as time goes by, due to the short life of their manufacturing company.

"CHARLAMAGNE"

FIRST KNOWN YEAR OF PRODUCTION **c. 1903/4**
MANUFACTURER **Ideal Toy and Novelty Company**
COUNTRY OF ORIGIN **USA** HEIGHT **51 cm (20 in)**

Ideal was the first of the American bear manufacturers. Early examples of bears produced by this company are very elusive and difficult to authenticate. The appearance of Ideal bears is, however, quite distinctive, and they are very appealing and collectible.

It should be possible to find bears from this era in good condition and not too expensive when compared with German bears of the same genre.

COLUMBIA BEAR

FIRST KNOWN YEAR OF PRODUCTION **c. 1907**
MANUFACTURER **Columbia Teddy Bear Manufacturers**
COUNTRY OF ORIGIN **USA** HEIGHT **43 cm (17 in)**

The early formative years of bear manufacturing provide the serious collectors with their greatest challenge and, needless to say, expense. Fortunately, many top quality bears have survived, including this "Laughing Roosevelt" bear from Columbia Teddy Bear Manufacturers.

These bears are still to be found today, albeit with great difficulty. However, an interesting feature of the "Laughing Roosevelt" bear is that the mouth can be operated by squeezing the stomach.

BRIGHT EYES BEAR

FIRST KNOWN YEAR OF PRODUCTION **c. 1917**
MANUFACTURER **The Stuffed Toy Company**
COUNTRY OF ORIGIN **USA** HEIGHT **43 cm (17 in)**

This Bright Eyes Bear was distributed by A. S. Ferguson & Company, under the name of Uncle Remus Stuffed Toys. Uncle Remus produced bears with a special patented eye-fixing method which ensured "permanent uniformity" in positioning the eyes and retaining the head shape. This eye-fixing method could have been based on Charles Sackman's invention, patent 844,619 in November 1908.

"*STILL HOPE*"

FIRST KNOWN YEAR OF PRODUCTION **c. 1907/8**
MANUFACTURER **Aetna Toy Animal Company**
COUNTRY OF ORIGIN **USA** HEIGHT **Unknown**

The Aetna Toy Animal Company, established in 1906, were probably the best American bear maker in the early days, as can be seen from this lovely example.

If you are interested in collecting or studying these bears, look for the printed oval trademark "AETNA", usually stamped across the centre of the bear's left foot pad, quite often indistinct, although traces can usually be found if you look carefully enough.

These bears, with their delightful appealing faces are quite wonderful. They are rare and extremely hard to find because the firm only existed for around two years.

IDEAL BEAR

FIRST KNOWN YEAR OF PRODUCTION **1908**
MANUFACTURER **Ideal Toy and Novelty Company**
COUNTRY OF ORIGIN **USA** HEIGHT **40 cm (15¼ in)**

This bear marked the end of an era for the Ideal Toy and Novelty Company.

Unfortunately they were only able to sustain the quality and style of their bears for about five years. For quite some time they adopted similar designs, and to some extent this detracts from their collectibility.

"CHRISTIAN GABRIEL"

FIRST KNOWN YEAR OF PRODUCTION **c. 1903/4**
MANUFACTURER **Margarete Steiff**
COUNTRY OF ORIGIN **Germany** HEIGHT **38 cm (15 in)**

Without doubt, Margarete Steiff is the world's leading manufacturer. Although its bears are highly desirable, they are likely to be extremely difficult to find and expensive.

Rod bears, such as the one featured here, are among the most collectible of early Steiffs, especially those with the original wax nose. In fact, should you own any of the early Steiff bears, you could be looking at a fortune.

Look out for the rarer colours (white and cinnamon) and one with its original button in the left ear, but remember that these bears will consistently attract a premium price.

"PAB 43" AND "PAB 35"

FIRST KNOWN YEAR OF PRODUCTION **1905**
MANUFACTURER **Margarete Steiff**
COUNTRY OF ORIGIN **Germany** HEIGHT **Unknown**

This PAB 43 from 1905 is shown here with a modern replica of a PAB 35. The original bear marked a successful change of direction for Steiff. If you are lucky enough to find one of the first PAB soft-filled bears, then it will cost you a considerable amount of money today.

Other rare bears from the Steiff collection include black bears (only a small number were made around 1910–12), the hot-water bottle bear (only 90 were made between 1907 and 1914), or unusually coloured bears.

Keep a sharp eye out for centre seam bears (1904–1906), which have wonderful faces and are well regarded. Again, they will also be expensive and scarce.

"STEIFF BEAR"

FIRST KNOWN YEAR OF PRODUCTION **c. 1907/8**
MANUFACTURER **Margarete Steiff**
COUNTRY OF ORIGIN **Germany** HEIGHT **40 cm (15¼ in)**

This perfect example of a Steiff bear was made at the height of the company's early success. A bear such as this one, with its cinnamon-coloured fur, is extremely rare and because of this, it will always attract a premium price.

Beware of imitation Steiff bears. Another company called Wilhelm Strunz, who operated at about the same time as Steiff, copied their products. It is anticipated that the bears are of inferior quality and construction.

If you are fortunate enough to own one of the bears featured above, or if you have a Richard Steiff grey teddy bear, then you could be looking at an absolute fortune.

"SERGEANT CULVER"

FIRST KNOWN YEAR OF PRODUCTION **c. 1907/8**
MANUFACTURER **Unknown** COUNTRY OF ORIGIN **Unknown**
HEIGHT **55 cm (20 in)**

This splendid costumed bear remains a mystery as far as the manufacturer and country of origin is concerned. His costume suggests that he was designed as a commemorative toy dating back to the American Civil War. This bear and its regalia are in excellent condition. Look at the tiny trumpet hanging from his left arm. The care and craftsmanship that has gone into making this characterful bear is truly amazing.

If you discover a bear such as this one and want to find out its origins, then there are a number of specialist dealers who are capable of providing a reliable advisory service including valuation and identification.

"EDELWEISS BEAR"

FIRST KNOWN YEAR OF PRODUCTION **c. 1909**
MANUFACTURER **Margarete Steiff**
COUNTRY OF ORIGIN **Germany** HEIGHT **40 cm (16 in)**

This unusual-coloured "Edelweiss" bear was made by
Steiff in the early 1900s. Note the metal button in the left
ear inscribed "STEIFF" with "FF" underscored. The nickel-
plated Steiff elephant button is supposed to have been the
first unregistered trademark "Knopf im Ohr". It was
followed by a blank button and then in 1905 by a button
embossed with "STEIFF", as shown on this example.

This bear will attract a high price because of its perfect
condition and the fact that it is complete with the metal
button in the left ear. The interesting silvery colour of its
coat also adds to its rarity.

"CINNAMON STEIFF"

FIRST KNOWN YEAR OF PRODUCTION **c. 1905**
MANUFACTURER **Margarete Steiff**
COUNTRY OF ORIGIN **Germany** HEIGHT **40 cm (16 in)**

Another characterful bear from Steiff, again with the unique
cinnamon-coloured fur. Centre seam bears, such as this
one, have wonderful faces and are highly regarded by
collectors.

Steiff have produced some of the most popular and
appealing bears throughout the ages.

23

"CENTRE SEAM STEIFF"

FIRST KNOWN YEAR OF PRODUCTION **c. 1905/6**
MANUFACTURER **Margarete Steiff**
COUNTRY OF ORIGIN **Germany** HEIGHT **40 cm (15¼ in)**

Here is a perfect example of the popular centre seam Steiff bear. Its characterful face and well-rounded body are typical of this type of bear. As with all bears manufactured by the Steiff company, this one is extremely rare and therefore, highly collectible.

If you particularly like the style of the Margarete Steiff bears (and they are very well-made and quite appealing), then you may be interested to visit the Margarete Steiff Museum in Germany, see page 80 for addresses of bear museums. You may also like to contact the manufacturers, as there is a Steiff Club for particular fans of these bears.

Steiff bears are fairly easy to identify as they are so distinctive, but if you are thinking of buying one, then always seek out a reputable dealer.

"WHITE STEIFF"

FIRST KNOWN YEAR OF PRODUCTION **c. 1907/8**
MANUFACTURER **Margarete Steiff**
COUNTRY OF ORIGIN **Germany** HEIGHT **56 cm (22 in)**

White Steiffs, such as the one shown here, are very collectible. They are extremely rare and, as a consequence of this, will always attract a higher market price.

Serious Steiff collectors should think about getting their bears catalogued and properly insured. This is not as expensive as you might think, and even though much of your collection might be irreplaceable, at least adequate insurance will be some recompense.

Carefully list as much information as possible about your bears – date of purchase, cost, size, make, and so on. You could get a valuation by an independent teddy bear specialist, depending on how valuable your collection is, and how comprehensive your records are. Photographing or videoing valuable bears is an alternative consideration.

"MASTER TEDDY"

FIRST KNOWN YEAR OF PRODUCTION **c. 1915**
MANUFACTURER **Leon Rees & Company**
COUNTRY OF ORIGIN **UK** HEIGHT **25½ cm (10 in)**

In 1915 at their Chiltern Toy Works, L. Rees & Co. produced the original Chiltern bear – "Master Teddy". This rather curious rotund fat-headed little teddy had googly eyes, was dressed in a pink and white striped shirt with large bib-type collar, ribbon bow tie and very high-waisted blue pants with a patch. It has a little red tongue.

The bear appears to have been available in five sizes, and although rare, they do exist; good quality ones are expensive, however.

The first advertisements (1915) indicate that the patch was on the left leg and without a chest tag, but bears with a patch on the right leg have been seen. Also around are bears with a chest tag indicating "US patent applied for"; these would have been made a year or two later.

"BING BEAR"

FIRST KNOWN YEAR OF PRODUCTION **c. 1910**
MANUFACTURER **Gebrüder Bing**
COUNTRY OF ORIGIN **Germany** HEIGHT **40 cm (15¼ in)**

The Gebrüder Bing firm made highly desirable bears which are surprisingly far scarcer than those produced by Steiff at the time. Expect to pay high prices for these bears, especially those that are still in good condition.

The desirable Bing Bear featured here still has its original silver button under its left arm. The button is inscribed with the letters "GBN" and any bear found with this button, or an orange-coloured button under its left arm, suggests a period between 1910 and 1919.

Any early Bing teddy bears, especially those made from unusual coloured mohair rather than the more conventional light to dark browns, will always be a great attribute to any collection.

"FARNELL BEAR"

FIRST KNOWN YEAR OF PRODUCTION **c. 1925**
MANUFACTURER **J. K. Farnell**
COUNTRY OF ORIGIN **UK** HEIGHT **50 cm (19½ in)**

This Farnell bear is a typical example, with the distinctive webbed claws and cardboard inserts in canvas feet. The Farnell webbing is quite different from that used by Merrythought and others of the time, and can easily be recognized by the pronounced triangular shape in the centre of their stitching.

Farnell always labelled their teddy bears using both their name, country of origin and the trade name, which was "Alpha Toys".

Look out for the early "Alpha" bears produced in the 1920s; the large bears are the best, always made using the top-quality mohair, and filled with excelsior or kapok or a mixture of both. Another indication of Farnell bears produced around this time is the dark blue embroidered lettering on a creamy base.

"FARNELL BEAR"

FIRST KNOWN YEAR OF PRODUCTION **c. 1925**
MANUFACTURER **J. K. Farnell**
COUNTRY OF ORIGIN **UK** HEIGHT **41 cm (16 in)**

The bear shown above is one of the new style of designs from J. K. Farnell, that appeared after the factory fire in 1934.

If you look at the bottom footpad of the bear, you can see the distinctive labelling that was always used. The body shape of this bear is similar to the bear shown above, although this particular bear seems to have adopted a rather worried-looking expression!

At this time there were a large number of teddy bear manufacturers around the world, which means that you have a good chance of finding quality bears from this era. Earlier bears, such as this one, made by one of the more famous producers, tend to be much more expensive.

"KNICKERBOX BEAR"

FIRST KNOWN YEAR OF PRODUCTION **c. mid 1930**
MANUFACTURER **Knickerbox Toy Company Incorporated**
COUNTRY OF ORIGIN **USA** HEIGHT **43 cm (17 in)**

The Knickerbox Toy Co. Inc. had been established for around 70 years when it began manufacturing teddy bears in the 1920s. The bears are recognizable by their very wide heads and short snouts. Some of the early bears had metal noses, and others had more conventional noses.

Despite the facial repairs, the bear shown above is a good example of a Knickerbox bear. Velveteen pads were used on these bears and the firm seemed to like coloured glass eyes, usually green. Pale yellow cloth labels were stitched onto the chest seam with a horseshoe logo inscribed "Knickerbox Toy Co. – New York".

By far and away the best of the American bears made during this era, Knickerbox bears remain relatively inexpensive when compared to others.

"CHAD VALLEY BEAR"

FIRST KNOWN YEAR OF PRODUCTION **c. early 1920s**
MANUFACTURER **Chad Valley Company Limited**
COUNTRY OF ORIGIN **UK** HEIGHT **71 cm (28 in)**

Under the banner of Chad Valley were a number of toy factories, but the teddy bears were made at the Wellington (Shropshire) factory.

Look out for lovely character bears such as the one shown here with its large triangular nose and distinctive blue button at the throat. Be careful about dates: a bear very reminiscent of this one was also advertised in 1935.

One way to tell a bear's age is by the buttons used by Chad Valley (if fitted). During the early 1920s, they had a broad steel rim with a flat recessed celluloid centre. "Chad Valley" buttons are coloured blue and may be found attached to either the bear's right ear, back or throat.

"CHAD VALLEY BEAR"

FIRST KNOWN YEAR OF PRODUCTION **c. 1923/4**
MANUFACTURER **Chad Valley Company Limited**
COUNTRY OF ORIGIN **UK** HEIGHT **43 cm (17 in)**

The Chad Valley bear shown here has the old cream-coloured Aerolite trademark button in its ear. The "Aerolite" button is usually found on the bear's right ear and is one way to tell its age.

Chad Valley changed the old steel rimmed buttons at about this time to cream-coloured or blue buttons, with raised centres, which were slightly convex. As with all Chad Valley bears, this one is full of character.

Chad Valley constantly took over other toy companies either to improve the line or to get rid of the competition. At about the same time as this bear was manufactured, it took over Isaacs & Co., whose well-known trademark for stuffed toys (usually on wheels) had been ISA.

"MERRYTHOUGHT BEAR"

FIRST KNOWN YEAR OF PRODUCTION **c. 1930s**
MANUFACTURER **Merrythought Limited**
COUNTRY OF ORIGIN **UK** HEIGHT **Unknown**

Some of the early Merrythought bears have similar distinguishing features to bears produced by other firms, particularly Chad Valley. The two companies had their factories only a few miles apart and one of their directors had previously worked for Chad Valley Company Limited.

Try to add to your collection Merrythought's early "M" range of "Magnet" bear as it was also known. The one shown here – probably from the "M" range – has a new nose, but it has its wishbone button and foot label. The button was usually fitted to the left ear, but occasionally it can be found on the back of the bear.

About this time Merrythought also introduced a webbing pattern applied to the hand paws. This is a much flatter web formation than the earlier Farnell method and only has "four fingers".

"CHILTERN SKATER BEAR"

FIRST KNOWN YEAR OF PRODUCTION **c. 1920s**
MANUFACTURER **H. G. Stone & Company Limited**
COUNTRY OF ORIGIN **UK** HEIGHT **33 cm (13 in)**

This adorable "skater" bear was made by Chiltern in the late 1930s. The muff and hat are original. As with all Chiltern bears, this one has a large nose with upturned, elongated outer stitching.

Labels from this period are similar to the first swing-type labels, but more decorative, with two houses in the left foreground of the typical rolling hills scene, but they are inscribed with the words, "trademark" (top), "Chiltern Toys" (centre), and "Made in England" at the bottom. These labels were used well into the 1950s.

In your search for rare Chiltern bears, look out for the "Cubby" (baby) line of bears introduced in 1930.

"CHILTERN HUGMEE BEAR"

FIRST KNOWN YEAR OF PRODUCTION **c. 1920s**
MANUFACTURER **H. G. Stone & Company Limited**
COUNTRY OF ORIGIN **UK** HEIGHT **56 cm (22 in)**

The Chiltern line of "Hugmee" bears from the early 1920s and early 1930s are the real finds and the most desirable. Beautiful coloured, fine-quality mohair was used, and filled with a mixture of excelsior and kapok, the bear truly lived up to its name, "Hugmee".

Note the distinctive "Hugmee" face and body of the bear shown above, which is a rare Chiltern bear from the late 1920s. The bears had flat feet with velveteen pads reinforced with cardboard. Squeakers were often inserted, but they are usually inoperable.

Swing-type labels were attached to the bears, but you will be extremely lucky to find them still in place. The circular trademark helps to identify the period. The first bears (1923–6) have "Chiltern" at the top with an outline of rolling hills centrally located and overprinted with "Toys" and the trademark at the bottom.

"DEANS BEAR"

FIRST KNOWN YEAR OF PRODUCTION **c. late 1930s**
MANUFACTURER **Deans Rag Book Company Limited**
COUNTRY OF ORIGIN **UK** HEIGHT **43 cm (17 in)**

It is surprisingly difficult to find Deans bears from this period, particularly those in good condition.

Deans bears tend to have a distinctive triangular-flat-shaped head with wide-set, almost vertically located ears, which distinguishes them from other British bears.

Sadly Deans bears may have been made from inferior quality mohair, which might explain why the bears are nearly always found with badly worn fur.

"FARNELL BEAR"

FIRST KNOWN YEAR OF PRODUCTION **c. 1920s**
MANUFACTURER **J. K. Farnell**
COUNTRY OF ORIGIN **UK** HEIGHT **58 cm (23 in)**

The odd proportions of this 1920s Farnell bear suggest that the head and body came from totally different bears! Looking at the bear's left arm, which has been considerably repaired, it would seem that this particular teddy has been well-loved over the years.

You can see the distinctive webbing on the paws, which is quite unlike that used by Merrythought and other companies of the time. It can easily be recognized by its pronounced triangular shape.

Dark blue embroidered lettering on a creamy base is indicative of Farnell bears from this era.

"CHAD VALLEY/ PEACOCK BEARS"

FIRST KNOWN YEAR OF PRODUCTION **c. mid 1930s**
MANUFACTURER **Chad Valley Company Limited**
COUNTRY OF ORIGIN **UK** HEIGHT **63 cm (25 in) & 93 cm (27 in)**

In 1931 Chad Valley acquired Peacock & Co., who had previously manufactured printed blocks. The sitting bear shown is made by Peacock. The Peacock range was really a Chad Valley bear with a different label with different wording to the original.

Peacock emblems are also known to exist on earlier labels. It is believed that the Peacock bears were made in the Chad Valley factory. These bears are rather scarce and a real find.

In 1938 Chad Valley was awarded a royal warrant and carries an appropriate wording on its labels. Any Chad Valley bears from this time are worth collecting, if in good condition, and they should not be too expensive.

"CHAD VALLEY BEAR"

FIRST KNOWN YEAR OF PRODUCTION **c. 1930**
MANUFACTURER **Chad Valley Company Limited**
COUNTRY OF ORIGIN **UK** HEIGHT **40½ cm (16 in)**

This is a typical Chad Valley bear produced around 1930. Note the distinctive bulbous nose and the red label. Later in the 1930s red lettering embroidered on a white label was introduced, along with bears who had large oval as opposed to bulbous noses. If you are lucky enough to find one of these versions, they are great characters to add to your collection.

"MERRYTHOUGHT BINGIE"

FIRST KNOWN YEAR OF PRODUCTION **c. mid 1930**
MANUFACTURER **Merrythought Limited**
COUNTRY OF ORIGIN **UK** HEIGHT **25 cm (10 in) & 30 cm (12 in)**

These two Merrythought "Bingies" come from a line that
was produced between 1931 and 1938. "Bingies" were
added to the range in 1931 and the seated bear pattern
proved to be so successful that it continued to be made for
several years, ending in 1938.

In your hunt for a "Bingie" to add to your bears, you will
come across some "Bingies" that are dressed. They often
had cloth bodies and limbs to save manufacturing costs.
The trademark label for these bears is to be found attached
to the inside of the lower left leg. Right from the start
Merrythought adopted a labelling system of black
lettering embroidered on a yellow background,
which was put on the sole of either foot. The typical
webbing pattern applied to the hand paws can be
seen here, which is a much flatter formation than early
Farnell bears.

"LINES BROTHERS (PEDIGREE) BEAR"

FIRST KNOWN YEAR OF PRODUCTION **c. 1938**
MANUFACTURER **Lines Brothers/International Model Aircraft Company Limited**
COUNTRY OF ORIGIN **UK** HEIGHT **53 cm (21 in)**

The Lines Brothers/International Model Aircraft Company
Limited (1937) produced the first "Pedigree" line of stuffed
toys in 1937. In 1938, "Pedigree" advertised a teddy bear
in its line, and this appears to be the first occasion that it
produced bears. The bear shown above is from a line that
continued to be produced until the 1950s.

During this period British companies were able to
establish themselves as equal to any of their foreign rivals.
At this time there were a large number of high-quality
teddy bears being produced and you stand a good chance
of being able to add a "Pedigree" bear to your collection.

"*MERRYTHOUGHT COLOURED BEAR*"

FIRST KNOWN YEAR OF PRODUCTION **c. mid 1930s**
MANUFACTURER **Merrythought Limited**
COUNTRY OF ORIGIN **UK** HEIGHT **23 cm (9 in)**

This unique bear was produced by Merrythought in the mid-1930s. Note the unusual colours of the overall body fur and also, the paw pads. The bear still has its distinctive Merrythought button and foot label, which adds to its value.

At about this time bright orange felt was often used for pads, although of course other colours were also used. The button in the bear's ear is similar to the one used by Chad Valley, but yellow with a wishbone trademark and overwritten "Hygienic – Merrythought – Toys". Usually the button was attached to the left ear of the bear, as seen here, although occasionally it can be found on the back of the bear.

"*CHILTERN HUGMEE*"

FIRST KNOWN YEAR OF PRODUCTION **c. 1930**
MANUFACTURER **H. G. Stone & Company Limited**
COUNTRY OF ORIGIN **UK** HEIGHT **60 cm (24 in)**

The Chiltern "Hugmee" was one of the finest quality character British bears ever produced and was made for over 50 years from 1923 onwards. You can see the fine-quality mohair which has been used for the coat of the bear featured here.

If you have one of these bears in your collection, hold on to it, for it is a real find and most desirable to collectors. This bear truly invites a hug and certainly lives up to its name. Once purchased or inherited, it is highly unlikely that a bear such as this one would ever leave a family, but would be more likely to be handed down from generation to generation.

The velveteen paws and characterful face are in extremely good condition.

"*SCHUCO BEAR*"

FIRST KNOWN YEAR OF PRODUCTION **c. 1935**
MANUFACTURER **Schuco (Schreyer & Company)**
COUNTRY OF ORIGIN **Germany** HEIGHT **9 cm (3½ in)**

A superb example of quality and character can be seen in this large Schuco bear, which dates back to the mid-1930s. Note the three-pawed hands and the feet, which are typical of all Schuco bears.

You may be interested to look out for the tiny little teddy bears produced by Schuco in the 1920s. The fashion at the time was for ladies to carry small purse-type handbags. Consequently all cosmetics had to be similarly small. Schuco came up with the novel idea of creating tiny teddy bears to carry all the essentials – there was even a whisky flask for gentlemen! These bears, from the "Piccolo" range, remain a delightful find for any collector, but in good condition they will not be cheaply priced!

Miniature mechanical clockwork tumbling bears, though lacking in bear character, are also great fun for collectors.

"*PETSY STEIFF*"

FIRST KNOWN YEAR OF PRODUCTION **c. 1927/8**
MANUFACTURER **Margarete Steiff**
COUNTRY OF ORIGIN **Germany** HEIGHT **43 cm (16½ in)**

This Steiff bear is from a range known as "Remembering Lou". Blue-eye "Petsy" bears are very difficult to find. Note the centre seam and tipped mohair on this example.

The "Petsy" range was introduced by Steiff in 1927 and was offered in ten sizes. The distinctive centre-seam patterned head was available in tipped mohair and plain gold colours. Of these, the beautiful blue-eyed two-tone mohair bears are definitely the most sought after.

Produced at about the same time was the "Teddy Baby", which came in 11 sizes and was made in many different guises, some with open or closed mouths.

These are also very popular with collectors, as are a considerable number of small bears from the time, created by Steiff.

"B ING - W ERKE B EAR"

FIRST KNOWN YEAR OF PRODUCTION **c. 1923/4**
MANUFACTURER **Gebrüder Bing**
COUNTRY OF ORIGIN **Germany** HEIGHT **58 cm (23 in)**

In 1920 Bing were to change their name to Bing-Werke and therefore the "GBN" button mark previously used was replaced by an orange button with the letters "BW" painted in black. By this time the button had been transferred from the body and attached to the outside of the bear's arm.

Many of the bears manufactured during the previous decade were now reproduced with some changes to the faces during the 1920s. The bears seen here, with their long snouts, are very distinctive of the period.

Sadly, Bing went out of business in 1932, and this of course makes their bears even more attractive to collectors. Some can be found complete with their button, which is an added bonus.

"W HITE S TEIFF B EAR"

FIRST KNOWN YEAR OF PRODUCTION **c. 1923/4**
MANUFACTURER **Margarete Steiff**
COUNTRY OF ORIGIN **Germany** HEIGHT **61 cm (24 in)**

At the time of commencement of the red linen ear tag (1925–34), Steiff were producing some really nice, original bears and these are easily distinguishable from the earlier versions. Their faces were now much slimmer, although still pointed, the back hump was far less pronounced and coloured glass eyes were used. This lovely white Steiff is a good example of how Steiff's range and style changed significantly after the mid-1920s.

Do look out for bears from around this period; often they can be found in good condition, but they can be rather expensive. Rare to find are the 1926 soft-filled "Teddy Clowns" – multi-coloured brown-tipped white mohair bears made in 11 sizes, along with a plain-coloured "Clown" yellow bear. This bear was made with two different neck ruffs, and those coloured white with blue borders are the most rare among them.

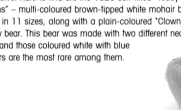

"SCHUCO YES-NO BEAR"

FIRST KNOWN YEAR OF PRODUCTION **c. 1930s**
MANUFACTURER **Schuco (Schreyer & Company)**
COUNTRY OF ORIGIN **Germany** HEIGHT **48 cm (19 in)**

Despite its new nose, there is no mistaking this Schuco Yes-No mechanism bear. Without doubt this is one of the most sought after and treasured lines. The bears can often be found in good condition because Schuco used only the finest quality materials. The "Yes-No Clown" is the rarest.

The "Bellhop" produced from 1921 is a real character bear, and if it is found with its red tunic, black pants, pillbox hat, and leather bag all perfectly intact, it is a must for any collection.

"PETER BEAR"

FIRST KNOWN YEAR OF PRODUCTION **c. 1926**
MANUFACTURER **Gebrüder Süssenguth**
COUNTRY OF ORIGIN **Germany** HEIGHT **33½ cm (13¼ in)**

Here is one of the delightful Peter bears made by Gebrüder Süssenguth. Needless to say, the fierce appearance of this bear was not popular with children of the time!

The "Peter" bear was one of the best known designs produced by this company.

"STEIFF BEAR"

FIRST KNOWN YEAR OF PRODUCTION **c. 1925/6**
MANUFACTURER **Margarete Steiff**
COUNTRY OF ORIGIN **Germany** HEIGHT **35 cm (13¾ in)**

This is a lovely example of a white Steiff bear. As with most unusual colours, these white bears are to be coveted as they are extremely valuable to collectors.

Look carefully at the bear's left ear and you will see the remains of a red tag still attached to the button.

"CHAD VALLEY BEAR"

FIRST KNOWN YEAR OF PRODUCTION **c. 1930s**
MANUFACTURER **Chad Valley Company Limited**
COUNTRY OF ORIGIN **UK** HEIGHT **55 cm (22 in)**

This unusual Chad Valley bear from the 1930s is made of white mohair and measures around 55 cm (22 in). Note the stitching on the feet of the bear and the long-angled stitching on the paws, which are typical of most bears from the Chad Valley range.

"STEIFF BEAR"

FIRST KNOWN YEAR OF PRODUCTION **c. 1925/6**
MANUFACTURER **Margarete Steiff**
COUNTRY OF ORIGIN **Germany** HEIGHT **61 cm (24 in)**

This Steiff bear was made after 1925, as can be seen from the remains of the red tag attached to the button. A bear such as this one will be highly valuable as it is in such good condition.

Later on, towards the beginning of the 1930s, the delightfully grinning bear called "Dicky" was produced. More usually this was made from gold mohair in eight sizes, with the rarer version in white available in five sizes. Around 1936 a cheaper version with inset snout and large feet was made for a few years. You will be very lucky indeed if you manage to find "Dicky" bears.

"Circus" bears, produced from 1936 until 1938, had snap joints and a neck mechanism enabling the bear's limbs and head to be set to pose. These bears remain some of the rarest examples from this whole era.

"EMIL TOYS BEAR"

FIRST KNOWN YEAR OF PRODUCTION **c. late 1930**
MANUFACTURER **Emil Toys**
COUNTRY OF ORIGIN **Australia** HEIGHT **40½ cm (16 in)**

In general, the indigenous teddy-bear manufacturers did not begin production until the late 1920s. One striking feature is the close resemblance between Australian bears and those produced by British manufacturers of the day.

Emil Toys came into being in the late 1930s and manufactured its bears in Victoria. The main distinguishing feature of these bears was their pugnacious appearance due to their large, round, permanently fixed heads set close to the shoulders, small ears, wide-set glass eyes, distinctive broad noses with pronounced elongated stitching, and long horizontal mouths.

This bear was made in the late 1930s and is recognizable as an Emil Toy bear by its fixed head.

"JOY TOYS BEAR"

FIRST KNOWN YEAR OF PRODUCTION **c. 1930**
MANUFACTURER **Joy Toys Pty**
COUNTRY OF ORIGIN **Australia** HEIGHT **61 cm (24 in)**

Australia's first teddy bear manufacturers were established in Melbourne in the late 1920s. For some years they struggled until around 1935 when they started to produce characters for Disney.

Joy Toys bears from this era used quality mohair and were usually softly filled with cotton flock except for the head, which used excelsior, occasionally this was also used for the rest of the bear.

A label sewn across the centre of the right foot rexine pad, was embroidered green on white, "Joy-Toys made in Australia". (Labels have also been found on the left foot.) The bear featured here is fully articulated unlike many other Australian bears. It closely resembles British bears from the same era.

"GEBRÜDER SÜSSENGUTH PETER BEAR"

FIRST KNOWN YEAR OF PRODUCTION **c. 1926**
MANUFACTURER **Gebrüder Süssenguth**
COUNTRY OF ORIGIN **Germany** HEIGHT **34 cm (13¼ in)**

This German company are reputed to have produced several bear designs, but the best known was "Peter" bear with its moveable eyes, tongue, and open mouth. The bear shown here is still in its original box. He has a disc attached to his chest inscribed with the words, "Peter – Ges.gesch – Nr 895257".

"Peter" bears were made in three sizes and colours, the most common of all being the brown-tipped mohair. It should have a white label with metal rim attached to its chest.

Collectors will be pleased to hear that it is still quite possible to find these interesting bears and recently, a small toy factory full of unopened boxed "Peters" was found.

"CHARACTER NOVELTY COMPANY BEAR"

FIRST KNOWN YEAR OF PRODUCTION **c. late 1940**
MANUFACTURER **Character Novelty Company**
COUNTRY OF ORIGIN **USA** HEIGHT **49 cm (19½ in)**

Unfortunately for collectors, the new safety rules so profoundly affected and restricted the design and manufacture of teddy bears that after 1960 they are generally lacking in character and appeal.

Character Novelty Company produced bears after the war and in the 1950s used the unusual technique of black button eyes applied to a white felt backing. The notable features on this bear are the shape and the felt pads behind the eyes.

Printed labels bearing the name "Character" were used, and which appear to have been sewn into the bear's left ear, as shown.

"KNICKERBOX BEAR"

FIRST KNOWN YEAR OF PRODUCTION **c. 1940**
MANUFACTURER **Knickerbox Toy Company**
COUNTRY OF ORIGIN **USA** HEIGHT **49 cm (19½ in)**

Like so many others, this popular American firm was producing bears based on its pre-war designs except that it seemed to prefer the shaven inset muzzle, rather like German firms of the time. The Knickerbox Toy Company produced some nice, good-quality bears during the late 1940s and 1950s, but very little else.

The Knickerbox bear shown here is from the 1940s and is one of the best examples of a postwar American teddy. Note the distinctive Knickerbox label on the chest. This bear is in particularly good condition.

"*C HAD V ALLEY B EAR*"

FIRST KNOWN YEAR OF PRODUCTION **c. 1950**
MANUFACTURER **The Chad Valley Company Limited**
COUNTRY OF ORIGIN **UK** HEIGHT **72 cm (28½ in)**

Many of the Chad Valley Company's first bears produced after the war were based on pre-war designs. Gradually, the wonderful character faces were sadly replaced by flat-faced, rather uninspiring teddy bears. The designers seemed to have lost their desire or perhaps ability to produce quality bears as the influence of pre-war bears disappeared. With perhaps one or two exceptions, Chad bears from this era do not attract much attention.

The Chad Valley bear shown here has the earlier Royal Warrant which reads, "HM the Queen". It was changed in 1953 to read "HM Queen Elizabeth the Queen Mother".

"*M ERRYTHOUGHT CHEEKY B EAR*"

FIRST KNOWN YEAR OF PRODUCTION **c. late 1950**
MANUFACTURER **Merrythought Limited**
COUNTRY OF ORIGIN **UK**
HEIGHT **38 cm (15 in) & 60 cm (24 in)**

The Merrythought firm continued to manufacture similar designs from the late 1930s, but it really took the "Punkinhead" bear, followed by "Cheeky" as shown here, to revive interest in the company.

Early versions of "Cheeky" bears should have the printed label with "Hygienic Toys" (centre) rather than the wording "Ironbridge, Shrops", which appeared from 1957 onwards.

"*LEFRAY BEAR*"

FIRST KNOWN YEAR OF PRODUCTION **c. mid 1950**
MANUFACTURER **Lefray Limited**
COUNTRY OF ORIGIN **UK** HEIGHT **53 cm (21 in)**

This British company was established in 1948. Lefray bears were typically British for the period, except for a very unusual standing bear made with a fixed body and strange face.

The individual-looking bear shown here was made to stand on very short fixed legs, but the head and arms are jointed. The ears are lined with brown velvet, and the nostrils are red in colour.

"*GEBRÜDER HERMANN BEAR*"

FIRST KNOWN YEAR OF PRODUCTION **c. 1956**
MANUFACTURER **Gebrüder Hermann**
COUNTRY OF ORIGIN **Germany** HEIGHT **41 cm (16 in)**

The Gebrüder Hermann company continued to make similar bears to those produced in pre-war times, but they also introduced a "Zotty" style at around the same time as Steiff. It is often hard to tell these bears apart.

If you want to distinguish between a "Zotty" and a Steiff bear from the time, the formation of the nose and mouth is quite different. The "Zotty" bear does not have a coloured bib and the eyes do not have felt backgrounds.

Look out for green and silver rosette-style hanging chest tags implemented in 1952, as shown above. If you find a bear with a circular pressed metal tag inscribed "Hermann-Teddy-Original", then you will know that bear was produced during the period 1941–51.

"WENDY BOSTON (c. 1945)"

Speak to anyone in the UK in their forties and they will probably tell you they were brought up on Wendy Boston bears produced during the 1950s and into the 1960s. The "Playsafe" nylon teddy could be thrown in the washing machine to emerge looking just as good as new.

These colourful one-piece bears came in all sizes and are now just beginning to be appreciated again. The picture below shows a representative range of Wendy Boston "Playsafe" bears from the late 1950s and 1960s.

Note that some bears have their labels on the right foot, which is normal, and some have labels on the left.

Look for bears with pinky white printed satin trademarks, usually sewn into the sole of the right foot. Even if the bears had been washed many times, you cannot mistake the label.

During the early 1950s Wendy Boston also made conventional jointed mohair teddy bears. These would be a good find for any collector.

"DEANS BEAR"

FIRST KNOWN YEAR OF PRODUCTION **c. 1955**
MANUFACTURER **Deans Rag Book Company Limited**
COUNTRY OF ORIGIN **UK** HEIGHT **51 cm (20 in)**

Deans Rag Book Company Limited was one of Britain's longest established toymakers. Although its famous cutout cloth patterns of teddy bears first appeared in 1908, it was not until 1915 that Deans made its first teddy bear.

In 1955 a remarkable new line based on real animals was introduced. This included a bear whose moulded face was overcovered with mohair, with moulded rubber hands and feet. There was a black bear, which imitated a real-life grizzly bear and off-white ones, as shown above, which were supposed to be polar bears. Both these types of bear are very scarce and therefore, highly collectible.

"FARNELL BEAR"

FIRST KNOWN YEAR OF PRODUCTION **c. 1964/5**
MANUFACTURER **J. K. Farnell & Company Limited**
COUNTRY OF ORIGIN **UK** HEIGHT **45 cm (17½ in)**

Some of the bears produced by Farnell during the early 1950s are well worth seeking out. Look for the blue and red printed label with a shield which was attached to bears made from 1940 to 1964.

In 1964, to coincide with the company moving to Hastings in Sussex, a plain printed label was used, "This is a Farnell Quality Soft Toy made in Hastings, England". Unfortunately, the bears never really lived up to the slogan.

The bear featured here is probably the last real character bear produced by Farnell. A label on the side of the body fixes the date of this bear to 1964/5.

"STEIFF BEAR"

FIRST KNOWN YEAR OF PRODUCTION **c. 1954/5**
MANUFACTURER **Margarete Steiff**
COUNTRY OF ORIGIN **Germany** HEIGHT **28 cm (11 in)**

If you look closely at the immediate post-war teddy bears, you can clearly see the relationship with those produced by Steiff ten or twenty years before. The slender faces are still quite distinctively Steiff, but the new era demanded changes which even Steiff could not avoid.

The 50th Anniversary bear produced in 1953 in three sizes called "Jackie" is likely to prove one of the best finds. The "Zotty" range of open-mouthed bears with distinctive, shaggy, frosted-tipped mohair and light-coloured chests were introduced in 1951. These are great fun to collect, offering lots of variety, but always try for those complete with ear tag and chest label. Look out for the rarest of all "Zotty" bears, which is the white one.

The bear shown above is a good example of how the original Steiff design became a little more rotund in 1952. Beware, however, when looking for Steiffs of this era, as many look-alikes were produced by other makers.

– OTHER GERMAN MANUFACTURERS –

PETZ COMPANY There is much confusion and contradictory information about this company. Some authorities suggest the firm existed and were making bears as early as World War I while others suggest they commenced after World War II. As yet we cannot be sure. Most of the Petz bears you are likely to find can be positively identified if they have the distinctive white glass, red-lettered, round trademark tag fixed to the chest, and these are likely to be from about 1946 onwards.

Other manufacturers known to have made bears during this period were: Clemens, Grisly Spielwaren, Althans KG, Anker, Baweku GmbH, Baumann & Kienel KG, EBO, Heunec and Hugo Koch.

"CHILTERN HUGMEE"

FIRST KNOWN YEAR OF PRODUCTION **c. early 1960s**
MANUFACTURER **H. G. Stone & Company Limited**
COUNTRY OF ORIGIN **UK** HEIGHT **68 cm (27 in)**

In the postwar recovery years the "Hugmee" bears still continued to be the tour de force in the Chiltern line, and the ones produced at the end of the 1950s/early 1960s are important examples to look out for.

There were now facial changes in the design, with the introduction of the unshaven snout, but the general body construction and shape remained very much the same. Plastic moulded noses were used circa 1958, and the ears then applied were a vertical floppy style.

The bear shown here is a later version of the Chiltern Hugmee. The ears lie flat on the head, and the face is slightly more pointed than before.

"CHILTERN MUSICAL STANDING BEAR"

FIRST KNOWN YEAR OF PRODUCTION **c. 1959/60**
MANUFACTURER **H. G. Stone & Company Limited**
COUNTRY OF ORIGIN **UK** HEIGHT **29 cm (1½ in)**

Favourite Chiltern bears of the time included the Ting-a-Ling Bear (1953) and the musical Baby Bruin (1958). These are rather similar bears except the latter (as shown here) had fixed legs to enable it to stand upright.

Printed labels, blue on white, were now glued to the sole of the right foot. These often became detached, but if you look, you can usually see where they were.

Red-printed labels were also used on some teddy bears, but these, along with similar-style blue labels, were usually sewn into the seam at the side of the body.

"LINDEE TOYS BEAR"

FIRST KNOWN YEAR OF PRODUCTION **c. 1950s**
MANUFACTURER **Lindee Toys**
COUNTRY OF ORIGIN **Australia** HEIGHT **50 cm (20 in)**

Lindee Toys was established in Sydney during the late war years and the company produced a variety of typically Australian teddy bears. During its early period it made a rather attractive musical bear with a distinctive moulded rubber nose and unusual teardrop-shaped rexine pads.

The appealing bear featured here was made in the 1950s. Note the moulded rubber nose and the tear-shaped rexine foot pads.

The trademark to look out for is an unusual red painted on white seated deer with the words, "Lindee Toys" inscribed inside.

"VERNA BEAR"

FIRST KNOWN YEAR OF PRODUCTION **c. 1950s**
MANUFACTURER **Verna**
COUNTRY OF ORIGIN **Australia** HEIGHT **75 cm (30 in)**

Although this Australian firm was established in 1941, it seems highly likely that due to wartime trade restrictions, it did not start manufacturing bears until around 1948.

Verna bears have a strong British influence, but look for the nose made of pieces of kidney-shaped felt. Foam-rubber moulding techniques were used for the heads, bodies and limbs, to which the fabric was applied. Verna bears were marked by a red embroidered on white label.

The foam-filled Verna bear shown here was made in the 1950s. Note the kidney-shaped black felt nose and the embroidered mouth.

"*B E R L E X   B E A R*"

FIRST KNOWN YEAR OF PRODUCTION **c. 1950s**
MANUFACTURER **Berlex Toy Pty**
COUNTRY OF ORIGIN **Australia** HEIGHT **51 cm (20 in)**

Quite when this Australian firm first started making bears is not clear, although they had been in operation since the 1930s. It is likely that it was probably some time in the 1950s because the bears are typical of that era, employing cheaper quality mohair.

Berlex adopted the fixed head style which was popular among many Australian bear-makers. Look out for the red printed on white label attached to either arm, and triangular stitched noses which Berlex favoured.

The head on this 1950s Berlex bear is fixed but the limbs are articulated. Note the triangular nose and the label on the left arm.

"*S C H U C O   B E A R*"

FIRST KNOWN YEAR OF PRODUCTION **c. 1950**
MANUFACTURER **Schuco (Schreyer & Company)**
COUNTRY OF ORIGIN **Germany** HEIGHT **44 cm (17½ in)**

Schuco bears made immediately after World War II are the most sought after of all those produced during Schuco's history. This company managed to keep up their pre-war standards, but bears in such good condition as the one above are very hard to find.

Without doubt the star of the Schuco range was a version of the earlier "Yes-No" bear called "Tricky". There was also a musical version made of this bear. Look for one with its red rosette-style plastic chest tag inscribed "Schuco Tricky". If it says "Made in US Zone Germany" on the reverse side, this predates the year 1953.

Another favourite bear, especially if you can find her fully clothed, is the lovely "Yes-No" girl dressed in flowered frock and pinafore. Most notable is the fact that the head, hands and feet were made of mohair and attached to an excelsior-filled fabric body, arms and legs. Schuco also continued their range of metal-bodied miniatures; pre-war miniatures had felt feet applied, but these were not used after the war, except, it is believed, on one very early 1950s bear.

" E MIL T OYS B EAR "

FIRST KNOWN YEAR OF PRODUCTION **c. 1950s**
MANUFACTURER **Emil Toys**
COUNTRY OF ORIGIN **Australia**   HEIGHT **51 cm (20 in)**

The bears manufactured by this Australian firm bore a remarkable similarity to those made by Joy Toys (see below), except Emil Toys bears always seem to lack any claw markings.

The bear featured here only has one eye, but its fixed-head and mohair fur will make it highly desirable to collectors. Note the elongated outer stitching on the nose.

Look for the label on the back or arm with a large letter "E" with a teddy bear on it to recognise an Emil Toys Bear.

" J OY T OYS B EAR "

FIRST KNOWN YEAR OF PRODUCTION **c. 1960s**
MANUFACTURER **Joy Toys Pty**
COUNTRY OF ORIGIN **Australia**   HEIGHT **38 cm (15 in)**

Many post-war Australian bear makers, including Joy Toys, still followed similar design concepts to the British manufacturers.

Although mohair had been extensively used, it was now replaced more and more by cheap synthetic plushes. The soft cotton flock filling was also dropped in favour of synthetic foam filling. The problem with the latter is that it deteriorates and crumbles easily with age. The bear shown above is a typical Australian bear from Joy Toys. It is filled with foam rubber.

Both the elongated, outer stitched nose and the green printed on white label were retained in post-war production by Joy Toys.

"HUG BEAR"

FIRST KNOWN YEAR OF PRODUCTION **c. 1983**
MANUFACTURER **North American Bear Company**
COUNTRY OF ORIGIN **USA** HEIGHT **47 cm (18 in)**

Barbara Isenberg created this American company in 1979, but it was the introduction of the Very Important Bear range (VIB) in 1980 that really caught the collector's eye. Based on famous celebrities, the range included Amelia Bearheart, Abearheim Lincoln, Bearlie Chaplin, Bearilyn Monroe and Elizabear Taylor with Richard Bearton, based on the film Cleopawtra.

"Hug", featured above, was designed by Ted Menten and was one of the North American Bear Company's early successes. Another hugely successful character bear range was the "Vanderbear" series and the "Muffy" series.

Initially preferred by American collectors, these bears are now appreciated in other parts of the world.

"ROSIE BEAR"

FIRST KNOWN YEAR OF PRODUCTION **c. 1993**
MANUFACTURER **Canterbury Bears**
COUNTRY OF ORIGIN **UK** HEIGHT **53 cm (21 in)**

Canterbury have produced large quantities of standard range bears in addition to limited editions especially for collectors, all of which are handmade by a loyal and dedicated workforce.

"Rosie", the bear featured, was designed by Maude and John Blackburn, who specialise in both special editions and standard ranges.

The Blackburns are great favourites on the American personal appearance circuit. Since 1991, they have collaborated with Gund Inc. of America to make a very special range of collectible limited editions for the USA.

"DELICATESSEN BEAR"

FIRST KNOWN YEAR OF PRODUCTION **c. 1987**
MANUFACTURER **House of Nisbet**
COUNTRY OF ORIGIN **Great Britain** HEIGHT **63 cm (25 in)**

Of all the contemporary manufacturers, the House of
Nisbet under the leadership of Jack Wilson were probably
the most adventurous. Jack Wilson cultivated an extremely
fruitful business relationship with the amazing Peter Bull,
resulting in the introduction of the "Bully Bear" range, and
the delightful edition of 12 "Zodiac" bears, based on a
book by Pauline McMillan and Peter Bull. It was a sad
loss to the teddy bear world when Jack decided to
retire in 1989 and the House of Nisbet was taken over
by Dakin.

"Delicatessen" ("Aloysius"), the bear shown here, is
another of Peter Bull's bears. It is without equal and this
design introduced distressed mohair, which artists have
since found so very helpful.

Limited editions, such as this one are now rather hard
to find, and they are a must for any serious collection.

"HEDDA HAIR BEAR"

FIRST KNOWN YEAR OF PRODUCTION **c. 1989**
MANUFACTURER **House of Nisbet**
COUNTRY OF ORIGIN **Great Britain** HEIGHT **40 cm (16 in)**

The following bears, produced in the Nisbet Celebrity
Collection, were limited to 5,000 of each design.

Yetta bear, Eric-Jon bear, Maybe and Wizard, all by
Carol-Lynn Rössell Waugh • Little Brown bear by Johnny
Gruelle • Pearly King bear by Doris and Terry Michaud •
Uncle Wiggily by Mabel R. Garis • The Bell Hop bear and
The Clown bear by April Whitcomb • Yes-No bear, based
on the Schuco method • Sir Freddy Farthing by Ted Menten
• Precious the Paper Doll bear by Peggy Jo Rosamond •
Mr Do-it-all bear by Linda Mullins • The Hedda Hair bear
by Lillian Rohaly • The Anything bear by Rosemary Volpp
• Theodore B. Bear and Victoria Bear, both by Beverley
Port • Red Mittens bear by Pat Schoonmaker • Grinnee
Bearit by Lucy Major • Gyles bear by Gyles Brandreth •
Drum Major bear by Dee Hockenberry • and Bentley
bear by Dakin.

Although listed in Nisbet's 1990 catalogue, the Jim
Ownby Tribute bear by Peggy Maxwell was apparently
never produced.

SPECIAL EDITION STEIFF BEARS

Spurred on by the need for a fresh approach to fight off the threat of cheap imports, Steiff introduced a special edition teddy bear in 1980 to commemorate the 100th anniversary of the company. Its success enabled them to implement state of the art production methods to reproduce the originals kept in the Steiff museum, which had also opened that year, as faithfully as possible, modern materials permitting.

Steiff regularly made exclusive limited editions for major department stores worldwide and also produced editions for Disney World and Disneyland Conventions held annually in the USA.

Many, but by no means all, of the Steiff replica bears have appreciated in value, some substantially which may be an inducement to some collectors.

ABOVE The larger Steiff bear from 1993 produced as a limited edition of 5000 (70 cm / 28 in).

ABOVE Steiff's 1990 replica of the world famous "Happy", looking as she would have done when new in 1926. She measures 65 cm / 26 in.

ABOVE One of five sizes of (unlimited) "Margaret Strong" gold bears introduced by Steiff in 1982. (60 cm / 23½ in).

"LAKELAND BEAR"

FIRST KNOWN YEAR OF PRODUCTION **c. 1991**
MANUFACTURER **Lakeland Bears/Little Folk**
COUNTRY OF ORIGIN **UK** HEIGHT **59 cm (23½ in)**

This attractively costumed plush bear, "heading for the hills" was the result of a collaboration between Lakeland Bears, who designed the outfits, and Little Folk.

From the outset in 1980, Little Folk realized that there was greater potential in the U.S., where most of its bears were exported. The very early designs used mohair, but this meant the bears were probably too expensive, and cheaper acrylic plush was successfully introduced circa 1982. This same line is produced today.

"GEBRÜDER HERMANN"

FIRST KNOWN YEAR OF PRODUCTION **c. 1984**
MANUFACTURER **Gebrüder Hermann**
COUNTRY OF ORIGIN **Germany** HEIGHT **Unknown**

Consistently one of Germany's mainstream teddy bear producers, Gebrüder Hermann entered the new specialist production market in 1984. This bear is a replica of a 1930s bear of theirs and was issued to commemorate Helen Sieverling's efforts to expand the teddy bear collector's knowledge.

"THE DESIGNER BEAR"

FIRST KNOWN YEAR OF PRODUCTION **c. 1991**
MANUFACTURER **Gebrüder Hermann**
COUNTRY OF ORIGIN **Germany** HEIGHT **57 cm (23 in)**

Like many other established firms, Gebrüder Hermann have produced bears based on their earlier designs that have been well received by collectors worldwide.

The "Anniversary" bear (1986), the "Designer" bear 1991, "Berlin Wall" bear (1991) and "Unification" bear (1991) are perhaps the best-known and favourite designs from this company.

The "Designer" bear featured here shows the character and quality of the limited edition bears produced by Gebrüder Hermann.

"CANTERBURY BEARS"

FIRST KNOWN YEAR OF PRODUCTION **c. 1991/3**
MANUFACTURER **Canterbury Bears**
COUNTRY OF ORIGIN **UK** HEIGHT **57/60 cm (23/24 in)**

Canterbury Bears, established in 1981 by John and Maude Blackburn, has grown from a small family group to a medium-sized outfit. Limited editions are handmade, especially for collectors, by a dedicated workforce.

The 10th Anniversary bear (100/500) shown here is embracing the special edition "Swallow", which is only one copy out of 25 that were made.

STEIFF LIMITED EDITION TEDDY BEARS

KEY TO SCARCITY FACTOR

1–3 currently available and easy to find
4–5 moderately easy to find
6–8 relatively difficult to find
9–10 very rare and expensive

NOTE: Until 1991, the last two numbers of the product code indicate size in cm. The EAN number, a European standard, was then introduced.

N/A = not applicable   W/W = worldwide

ABOVE "Jubilee" or "Papa" bear was the first modern limited edition, produced in 1980 (height 43 cm/ 17 in).

Year of Production		Replica Product Code	Description	Quantity	Scarcity Factor
Original	Replica				
1903	1980	0153/43	JUBILEE BEAR, but commonly known as PAPA BEAR	11,000 W/W (6,000 German certificate, 5,000 to USA, English certificate)	9–10
1903	1981	0155/38	MAMA AND BABY SET (Mama 40 cm/16 in, Baby 15 cm/6 in)	8,000 USA	9
N/A	1982	0203/00	ORIGINAL TEDDY WHITE SET	2,000 USA	9
N/A	1982	0204/17	TEA PARTY SET (4 dressed bears with tea set and scene)	10,000 USA	6–7
1905	1982/83	0150/32	RICHARD STEIFF GREY TEDDY BEAR	Unnumbered No certificate but tied-on booklet is signed. Estimates vary from 11,000 to 20,000 W/W	8
N/A	1983	0210/22	TEDDY ROOSEVELT COMMEMORATIVE SET or NIMROD or CAMP FIRE (4 small dressed bears with scene)	10,000 USA (Note: many sets were broken up and bears sold separately)	7
1904	1983	0160/00	MARGARET STRONG CHOCOLATE SET (4 different bears 18 cm/7 in, 26 cm/ 10½ in, 32 cm/12¼ in and 42 cm/17 in)	2,000 USA	8

Year of Production		Replica Product Code	Description	Quantity	Scarcity Factor
Original	Replica				
1904	1984	0156/00	Margaret Strong Cinnamon Set (4 different bears 18 cm/ 7 in, 26 cm/10½ in, 32 cm/ 12¼ in and 42 cm/17 in)	2,000 USA	8–9
1894	1984	0082/20	Roly-Poly Bear	9,000 W/W	4–5
1906	1984	0162/00	Giengen Teddy Set (Mother) 32 cm/12½ in with Baby in Cradle 10 cm/4 in)	16,000 W/W	6–7
N/A	1984	4003 (Large Set)	Goldilocks & 3 Bears Papa Bear 33 cm/13 in, Mama 30 cm/12 in, Baby 24 cm/9½ in. Doll by Susan Gibson	2,000 USA	7
N/A	1984	0225/42	Ophelia Bear from *Ophelia's World* by Michelle Durkson-Clise	USA Limited by time production (Note: Button but no tag)	7
1930	1985	0172/32	Dicky Bear	20,000 W/W	6
1905	1985	0085/12	Bear on Wheels	12,000 W/W	5
N/A	1985	4004 (Smaller Set)	Goldilocks & 3 Bears Papa Bear 23 cm/9 in, Mama 18 cm/7 in, Baby 12.5 cm/ 5 in and doll	5,000 USA	6–7
1904	1985	0158/25 0158/31 0158/41	Margaret Strong White (leather pads) (leather pads) (leather pads)	2,000 USA	8
1904	1986	0158/50	Margaret Strong White (leather pads) Large	750 USA	9–10
1926	1986	0170/32	Teddy Clown	10,000 W/W	7
1953	1986/7	0190/25	Jackie Bear (medium-size)	10,000 W/W	6–7
1913	1987	0164/31 0164/32 0164/33 0164/30	Circus Dolly Bears yellow green violet pale yellow (Note: blue and red also shown in catalogue but not produced)	5,000 USA initially, then W/W	6–7 6 6 9

BELOW "Teddy Rose", a centre seam replica, was made in 1987 and measures 41 cm/16 in and has many fans among collectors.

BELOW RIGHT "Jackie", a reproduction of the 1953 anniversary bear, was first made in 1988 and is shown here in all the sizes so far issued.

Year of Production		Replica Product Code	Description	Quantity	Scarcity Factor
Original	Replica				
1905	1987	0163/19	Teddy Clown Jr	3,000 USA with white tags (Note: 2,000 also issued with yellow tags)	8–9
1925	1987	0171/41	Teddy Rose	10,000 W/W	6–7
1907	1987	0227/33	Schnuffy	Limited by time production issued to USA but later about 300 released into UK (undressed) (Note: Button no tag)	7
N/A	1987	0131/00	Three Bears in a Tub butcher, baker and candle-stick maker in tub	1,800 USA	7–8
N/A	1988	0227/33	Baby Ophelia	Unstated limit USA. Only *Button* in ear	6
N/A	1988	0120/10	Bear Bandsman (Circus series)	5,000 USA	5–6

Year of Production		Replica Product Code	Description	Quantity	Scarcity Factor
Original	Replica				
1953	1988	0190/35	Jackie Bear (large)	4,000 W/W	5–6
1908	1988	0155/18	Roly-Poly Bear	3,000 USA	7
1908	1988	0174/46	White Muzzle Bear (medium-size)	5,000 USA	7–8
1907	1988	0173/40	Black Bear (with leather nose)	4,000 W/W	8–9
1924	1988	0132/24	Wig-Wam' Bear 2 small bears and pull-along seesaw	4,000 W/W	5–6
1907	1989	0174/61	British Collectors Series Bear (1st)	2,000 UK	9–10
1939	1989	0135/20	Baby Bear on Trolley	4,000 W/W	4–5
1931	1989	0130/28	Bear on All Fours	4,000 USA	6
1908	1989 reissued 1991 (USA)	0158/17	Snap-a-Part Bear	5,000 W/W	5–6
N/A	1989	0175/19	Teddy Bear Ringmaster	7,000 USA	4–5
N/A	1989	0163/20	Clown Teddy From golden age of the circus series	5,000 USA	5

LEFT This black bear (issued in 1987) caused a great furore when issued in the UK and because of small numbers, its priced trebled within a year (height 40 cm/15¾ in).

BELOW This "Snap-Apart" bear issued in 1989 measures 17 cm/ 6¾ in).

LEFT The "Petsy Brass" replica was issued in 1989 and measures 35 cm/13¾ in.

RIGHT This is the reproduction of the blue "Bi-colour Petsy" issued in 1989. It measures 50 cm/19¾ in.

YEAR OF PRODUCTION		REPLICA PRODUCT CODE	DESCRIPTION	QUANTITY	SCARCITY FACTOR
ORIGINAL	REPLICA				
1927	1989	0181/35	PETSY BRASS	5,000 W/W	6
1953	1989	0190/17	JACKIE BEAR	12,000 W/W	4
1927	1989	0180/50	BICOLOUR PETSY CENTRE SEAM	5,000 USA	6–7
1908	1989	0174/60	WHITE MUZZLE BEAR (large)	2,650 USA	9–10
1908	1990	0174/35	WHITE MUZZLE BEAR (small)	6,000 W/W	5
1926	1990	0169/65	HAPPY ANNIVERSARY REPLICA	5,000 W/W	8–9
1925	1990	0171/25	TEDDY ROSE (small)	8,000 W/W	5
N/A	1990	0177/19	TEDDY BEAR FOOD VENDOR (Circus series)	5,000 USA	4–5
1955	1990	0188/25	TEDDY WITH NECK MECHANISM	4,000 W/W	5–6
1909	1990	0164/29	SOMERSAULT BEAR	5,000 W/W	6–7
1906	1990	0174/33	BRITISH COLLECTORS SERIES BEAR (No 2)	3,000 UK	5–6
1913	1990	0116/25	RECORD TEDDY (on wheels)	4,000 W/W	7–8
N/A	1991	650529 (EAN)	TEDDY BEAR TICKET SELLER (Circus series)	5,000 USA	4–5
1903	1991	404108 (EAN)	35 PB REPLICA (50 cm/20 in) (in USA often referred to as "Baerle" bear)	6,000 W/W	8

Year of Production		EAN Numbers Used	Description	Quantity	Scarcity Factor
Original	Replica				
1926	1991	407215	Baby Happy Anniversary (40 cm/16 in) (Note: Box incorrectly states 5,000 limit but certificate is correct)	6,000 W/W	4–5
1912	1991	406096	British Collectors Series Black Bear (No 3) (33 cm/13 in)	3,000 UK	5–6
1908	1991	406119	Dark Brown Muzzle (35 cm/14 in)	5,000 USA	4–5
1913	1991	400704	Record Teddy Rose (on wheels)	4,000 W/W	3–4
1931	1991	408113	Yellow Teddy Baby (15 cm/6 in)	5,000 USA	4
1931	1991	408114	Yellow Teddy Bear (32 cm/12½ in)	5,000 USA (a few later released to UK)	4
N/A	1991	650529	Teddy Baby Ticket Seller (Circus series)	5,000 USA	4
1930s	1991	606106	Teddy Baby Watch Set (1st Issue – complete stand, bear and 13 watches)	2,000 W/W	8 Complete Set
1930s	1992	606304	Teddy Baby Watch Set (2nd Issue – complete stand, bear and 13 watches)	4,000 W/W	6–7

LEFT This group of white muzzled bears was issued between 1988 and 1990. The larger of these (60 cm/23½ in) is extremely hard to find. The other sizes are 35 cm/13¾ in and 46 cm/18 in. Most collectors remove the muzzles.

RIGHT The 35PB replica was issued in 1991. It reproduces the string joints and sealing wax nose (height 50 cm/ 19½ in).

BELOW This somersault or "Purzel" bear was issued in 1990 and measures 29 cm/ 11½ in. It uses a clockwork mechanism.

LEFT The British Collector's series always produces attractive bears. This brown bear was issued in 1993 (height 60 cm/24 in).

RIGHT Another in the British Collector's series issued in 1992 and measuring 40 cm/ 16 in.

YEAR OF PRODUCTION		EAN NUMBERS USED	DESCRIPTION	QUANTITY	SCARCITY FACTOR
ORIGINAL	REPLICA				
1911	1992	406645	BRITISH COLLECTORS SERIES WHITE BEAR (No 4) (Sometimes referred to as LOUISE in the UK) (40 cm/16 in)	3,000 UK	4–5
1928	1992	407482	YELLOW MUSICAL BEAR (40cm/16 in)	8,000 W/W	3–4
1930	1992	407550	WHITE DICKY BEAR (25 cm/10 in)	9,000 W/W	3
1930	1992	407574	WHITE DICKY BEAR (33 cm/13 in)	7,000 W/W	3
1912	1992	406805	SMALL BLACK BEAR (40 cm/16 in)	7,000 W/W	3–4
1912	1992	406774	"OTTO" 1st ISSUE NEW USA COLLECTORS SPECIAL (40 cm/16 in)	5,000 W/W	3–4
1974	1992	400872	SEESAW BEAR AND MONKEY (on wheels)	4,000 W/W	3
N/A	1992	038006 (WO38006)	NOAH'S ARK WITH MR AND MRS NOAH (20 cm/8 in) BEARS WITH BAMBOO ARK (Note: Wooden ark alternative offered in USA)	8,000 W/W	4
1905	1993	404207	BARLE 35 PAB (35 cm/14 in)	6,000 W/W	3–4
1926	1993	400919	UR TEDDY (20 cm/8 in)	4,000 W/W	1

YEAR OF PRODUCTION		REPLICA PRODUCT CODE	DESCRIPTION	QUANTITY	SCARCITY FACTOR
ORIGINAL	REPLICA				
1951	1993	408458	MUSICAL TEDDY (35 cm/14 in)	5,000 W/W	2
1907	1993	406010	TEDDY BEAR BROWN 1907 (70 cm/28 in)	5,000 W/W	4–5
1930	1993	407512	TEDDY BABY DRESSED GIRL	7,000 W/W	1
1930	1993	407529	TEDDY BABY DRESSED BOY	2,000 W/W	1
1907	1993	406065	BRITISH COLLECTORS SERIES LARGE BROWN (No 5) (60 cm/24 in)	3,000 W/W	4
1903	1993	650574	ALICE 2nd ISSUE USA SPECIAL COLLECTORS SERIES	5,000 W/W	3
N/A	1993	038327	BEAR SET FOR ARK SERIES (2 bears)	8,000 W/W	2
1929	1992/93	420016	STEIFF 1st ISSUE CLUB BEAR BLUE TEDDY BEAR (28 cm/11 in)	approx 7,500 issued outside USA	Available only to Steiff Collector Club members
N/A	1993/94	420023	STEIFF 2nd ISSUE CLUB BEAR TEDDY CLOWN (28 cm/11 in)	issued outside USA	Available only to Steiff Collector Club members
N/A	1993/94	420801	STEIFF USA 1st ISSUE CLUB BEAR — SAM	issued only in USA	Available only to Steiff Collector Club members USA only

LEFT The first USA Steiff Collector's Club issue in 1994 was a bear called "Sam" (height 28 cm/ 11 in).

RIGHT The European Collector's Club was introduced in 1993 and has been a huge success. The "Blue Teddy Baby" (28 cm/11 in) was an exclusive issue to club members.

STEIFF LIMITED EDITION TEDDY BEARS

LEFT The delightful "Teddy Clown" was made in 1986 and measures 32 cm/13 in. As with all Steiff collector's bears, it is handmade from the finest quality mohair.

RIGHT This small grey "Richard Steiff" was made in 1982/3 and measures 32 cm/13 in. It was based on Richard Steiff's prototype and is a great favourite with collectors.

ABOVE "Dicky" was produced in 1985 in a very large limited edition of 20,000, but its collectibility is now increasing (height 32 cm/13 in).

ABOVE The "Circus Dolly" bear, issued in 1987, was made in four colours. It was first distributed in the USA, followed by the rest of the world.

THE ERA OF THE TEDDY BEAR ARTIST

The trouble in trying to define the term "teddy bear artist" is that this is such a contentious and emotive subject, you inevitably alienate some people. Probably above all else the major feature which distinguishes the real teddy bear artist from all other crafts people or bear-makers, is the ability to create, without the conscious influence of others, a teddy bear of distinctive quality and character. It is not just a matter of good workmanship, however desirable this may be; the design concept must be original with a clear aesthetic quality and style.

Many people are perfectly competent bear-makers and their workmanship is consistent and precise, but they are simply incapable of instilling life in a bear, or, as our old friend Steve Schutt often says, "giving the bear a soul". An artist bear must be instantly recognizable as the work of a particular creator, just as most people can easily distinguish the work of, say, Van Gogh from a painting by old Aunt Mabel!

All artists have to be innovators, otherwise their work becomes mundane, rather than inspirational and a teddy that we simply must own. A true teddy bear artist will possess a wide-ranging repertoire, be adventurous and not afraid to disregard convention, and instinctively be able to produce everything from classical to whimsical and even occasionally unusual designs. The artist will seek out new materials, apply new techniques or concepts, and constantly diversify his or her designs, rarely being perfectly content with the result.

Where did bear artistry begin? The true origins of the teddy bear artist are somewhat obscure, although we only have

ABOVE Diane Gard (USA) based "Billy Ray" on an American football hero. He was made exclusively for the 1992 Walt Disney World Doll and Teddy Bear Convention.

to go back to the 1970s in the USA to find who were the guiding spirits and true pioneers of the movement.

Many of the early craft bear-makers and their successors were largely influenced by two English people. One was Margaret Hutchings, a journalist on one of the UK's leading newspapers, who in 1964 wrote the definitive teddy bear-making manual, *The Book of the Teddy Bear*. The other was of course Peter Bull.

The first teddy bear artist was the American, Beverley Port. From the 1970s Beverley guided and taught many of the current teddy bear artists. She had broken free from the traditional restraints and prejudices which had restricted her as a doll artist to pursue her new interest in teddy bear-making, encouraging a great many others by her example. She is recognized as the "mother" of teddy bear artistry.

In 1980, the Americans, Alan and Peggy Bialosky produced their book *Teddy Bears Catalogue* which provided added impetus and stimulus to those involved with teddy bears.

Carol-Lynn Rössell Waugh, herself an ex-doll maker, was one of the early disciples of this new movement. An art historian, she became a prominent authority on the subject and was probably the person who coined the term "teddy bear artist". She has written extensively over the years, promoting the work of artists, and has herself produced many fine bears, as well as designing for major manufacturers.

Another artist who was an undoubted inspiration and influence on the movement, not least because of his own designs, was Ted Menten. A photographer and author, his many wonderful teddy bear books have inspired others. His outrageous parody of *Harpers Bazaar* entitled *Teddy's Bearzaar* provided a unique opportunity for the invited artists to make special bears displaying their tremendous flair. The bears replaced the usual female models in the advertisements and articles to provide an absolutely wonderful, whimsical and funny book that has helped to open new horizons and, most importantly, validate artists and their bears as a highly collectible commodity.

Around 1982–3 in the USA many aspiring people became attracted to bear-making, and some with undoubted qualities began to emerge and develop their skills. Teddy bear shows were also being established which gave prominence to a new generation of bear-makers – real artists who brought to the art not only new and invigorating design concepts but a positive desire to create an artistic group or community. Among the many who became idealistically involved were Steve Schutt, Diane Gard, Joan Woessner, Anne Cranshaw and Denis

Shaw, who by their example epitomized integrity and strong ethical principles which bear artists were to find invaluable in the years ahead.

The foundations were laid for these instigators, and others, to encourage the sharing of ideas, knowledge and interaction with those of similar interests. The movement grew rapidly, resulting in the production of new and exciting teddy bears at a time when collectors were really hungry for something different, individual, and not too expensive. There was an immediate rapport with collectors which has grown and lasted to this day.

ABOVE Jo Greenco created "Miss Marple", based on Agatha Christie's famous detective, in 1993 (height 48 cm/19 in). Jo specializes in interesting characters from the past. They are usually kept to small limited editions or are one-off designs.

Subsequently, the influence of the American bear artist spread to other countries, in particular to Britain, while the Netherlands, Germany, Australia, New Zealand, and Japan are now beginning to develop their own artist bear markets.

American artists have given the lead which other new artists around the world should appreciate and, while still developing their own ideas, gladly follow. In Britain, the standard of artist teddy bears has improved enormously to the point where the creations of some potentially excellent artists are often equal to those produced by American artists; and this is now beginning to happen in other countries, too.

Without doubt, the artist bear is currently the vogue, and an enormous international market has developed which is presently the most important of the three genres (old, contemporary, and artists) covered in this book. This happened partly because of the high prices demanded for old bears, and partly because contemporary alternatives were becoming predictable and relatively far too expensive.

The tremendous variety, individuality, and quality provided by artist bears probably satisfies the needs of many present-day collectors, who are more sophisticated, well-informed, discerning, and demanding than those a decade ago.

GALLERY OF BEARS

Artists everywhere now produce store-specials, limited editions, one-of-a-kind bears, as well as charitable donations and show pieces. There is an exciting variety of bears available to collectors to suit all tastes and pockets. One of the appealing factors, however, is that the majority of artists abhor the idea of producing large numbers of the same bear. The restricted production greatly enhances future investment prospects; the one-of-a-kind bears and small-quantity editions are likely to be the rarities for future generations of collectors. Of course, anyone can make a single bear, but it is the special edition teddy bears produced by distinguished artists that are likely to prove the best investment prospects. However, no one can ever be quite sure what future generations of arctophiles will prefer, so why not just enjoy collecting artist bears regardless of their potential value?

ABOVE Billee Henderson (USA) is an award winning bear designer who can turn her hand to a range of styles. "James", a traditional bear, was made in 1993.

ABOVE Kathy Wallace (USA) has been making bears since 1982. Her designs are traditional and full of character. "German Gold" measures 62 cm/24½ in (1991).

ABOVE American Ena Hammond creates bears with distinctive personalities. Ena made "Woolly Bear" in 1991. He measures 30 cm/12 in.

ABOVE Anne Inman (USA) is renowned for her innovative ideas. "Strawberries and Cream" is filled with fragranced pellets! She was made in 1993 (height 48 cm/19 in).

LEFT "Lady Margaret" was made by one of America's top artists, Marcia Sibol, in 1991 (height 84 cm/33 in) especially for the authors. She is the gossip columnist of the Teddy Bear Times!

ABOVE Teresa Rowe is one of Britain's up and coming artists. The "Mad Hatter", a character from Alice in Wonderland, was made in 1994 and measures 30½ cm/12 in.

ABOVE Deborah Canham is one of Britain's best artists. These delightful circus bears (5 cm/2 in) were made in 1993.

ABOVE "Wizard" by Brenda Dewey (USA) c. 1993. He measures 13 cm/5 in and is typical of her Fantasy style. Diverse in size and inspiration, these bears are usually limited editions or one-offs.

ABOVE "Bearlin the White Wizard" by Kathryn Riley was created in 1993. Amazingly, he was only her third ever bear!

ABOVE Janet Clark has been making bears seriously for three years and is now one of Britain's top artists. "Loving" was made in 1994.

ABOVE "Elfinbeary Peach" (14/100) illustrates Joan Woessner's versatility and creativity and confirms her position as a top American artist (1992).

ABOVE Dee Hockenberry (USA), creator of "Mr Bruin" (1990, height 37 cm/13 in), is one of the world's leading authorities on old bears in addition to being a talented artist.

ABOVE "Jenny-Lynn" was made by Carol-Lynn Rössel Waugh (USA) in 1993 (height 50 cm/ 20 in). Carol-Lynn is a top artist in addition to being a prolific writer and an authority on teddy bear artistry. She has also designed bears for manufacturers.

ABOVE Anne Cranshaw's (USA) "Casco Bear" (1993, 37 cm/14½ in) is a captivating little bear created for Teddies of the World '93.

ABOVE "Antique Gray Bear" was made by Barbara Conley (USA) in 1993 using traditional style and methods (height 39 cm/15½ in).

ABOVE Lynda Graves (UK) prefers to make very small numbers of her character bears. "Stargazer" was made in 1993 in a limited edition of three. (Height 41 cm/16 in).

ABOVE Before turning her talents to artist bears, Pam Howells (UK) was a designer for Chiltern. "Charlotte" was made in 1993 and measures 58 cm/23 in.

ABOVE These delightful clown bears named "Cornetto" and "Pauro" were made by Shirley Latimer (UK) in 1993. They measure 38 cm/15 in and 9 cm/7½ in.

ABOVE "Marisa Bearensen" was made by Diane Gard in 1988 (height 60 cm/24 in). She was created for Ted Menten's parody of Harper's Bazaar. "Marisa" is dressed in her Yves St Bearant gown.

ABOVE Celia Baham (USA) is a prolific and very creative artist. The "Roosevelt Bear" shown is from her second edition. He was made in 1993 and measures 46 cm/18 in.

ABOVE Sue Quinn's popularity has spread from her native Britain to the rest of the world. "Sugar Plum Bear" was made in 1993 and measures 33 cm/13 in.

ABOVE "Debbie" is a teenager from the 1950s and a big Elvis fan, of course! She was made by Diane Gard (USA) in 1994 in a limited edition of ten and measures 75 cm/30 in.

ABOVE Rosalie Frischmann's (USA) bears are highly sought. "Murphy" was made in 1991 and measures 58 cm/23 in.

ABOVE Janet Clark's (UK) captivating bear and bunny called "Sophie" was made for the Teddies of the World '93 convention. (Height 55 cm/22 in).

ABOVE "Gerry's Teddy at Play" was created especially for the authors by Jane Humme of the Netherlands in 1993 (height 9 cm/3½ in).

LEFT Gregory Gyllenship is one of a handful of British male teddy bear artists. He prefers traditional designs, as can be seen from "Alexander" (seated) and "Gilbert." (Height 40½ cm/16in, 1993.)

ABOVE More appealing creations from Dee Hockenberry (USA). These are called "Timeless Teddies" and measure 30 cm/12 in and 35½ cm/14 in. They were made in 1993.

ABOVE There is precision and quality in Nancy Crowe's (U.S.A.) work. "Sandman" was made in 1993 and measures 36 cm/15 in.

ABOVE "Luke" is another example of the delightful, characterful bears being created by the talented Dutch artist Jane Humme. (Height 18 cm/7 in, 1993.)

ABOVE "Buster" by Brian Beacock (Britain) was made in 1987 and measures 50 cm/20 in. Dr. Brian is probably better known as a teddy bear restorer, but he has designed several bears for production.

ABOVE "Marvin the Magician" was made in 1993 by one of Britain's top artists – Naomi Laight. She rarely dresses her bears, but Marvin shows her skilful use of antique materials.

ABOVE "Huxley" by Denis Shaw (USA), is an appealing interpretation of a real bear. He was made in 1993 and measures 24 cm/9½ in.

ABOVE One of America's most successful artists, Janet Reeves makes bears in demand worldwide. "Miss Hildegard" was made in 1993 and measures 44 cm/ 17½ in.

ABOVE "Hans-Werner Jager" was made by the German artist Heike Gumpp (height 51 cm/ 20½ in). "The Hunter" illustrates Heike's wonderful eye for detail.

ABOVE "Emmett" is part of Steve Schutt's wonderful Bedy-By series. The long-limbed design is very distinctive. He was made in 1991 (height 36½ cm/ 14½ in).

ABOVE Composition pieces are always in demand. "The Strawberry Picker" by Linda Edwards (UK) is a stunning creation made in 1993 measuring 43 cm/17 in.

ABOVE These traditionally dressed bears, "Sumo bear Yokozuna" and "Kimono," were created by Japanese artist Terumi Nishiyama in 1993. (Height 13 cm/5 in.)

ABOVE The quality and detail of this delightful bear by Marcia Sibol (USA) speaks for itself. "Jenny" was made in 1991 and measures 37 cm/14½ in.

ABOVE "Pearly King and Queen" were made by Nicola Perkins (UK), a top miniaturist. These two traditional British characters measure 7½ cm/3 in.

ABOVE Mary Holden (UK) likes to keep her bears as environmentally friendly as possible by using natural wool fillings. "Baby George" measures 46 cm/18 in (1994).

WHERE AND HOW TO BUY BEARS

The problems facing every collector are what to collect and how much to spend. You have to decide whether collecting is purely to satisfy a love of bears, or whether it is a matter of investment. Both have quite different requirements. There are a whole host of possible sources of where to buy or sell teddy bears, all of which have advantages and, dare we say, pitfalls.

RARITY FACTOR

However popular they all may appear, it is obvious that some teddy bears are rarer than others, usually because very few were ever made. Sometimes rarity is assumed because it may be extremely difficult to attribute a bear of undoubted quality and appeal to a specific manufacturer. Fortunately, some manufacturers are well-known and particular items can be positively identified from company records and other reliable sources; Steiff are a prime example but even with them positive substantiation is sometimes difficult. All too often reliable information about a manufacturer is scarce or even non-existent. This fact creates an awful dilemma for those trying to determine authenticity.

The question of rarity is of little relevance if the particular teddy bear is so unattractive or crudely made that no one could possibly be interested. The law of supply and demand really determines the value of most bears, whether rare or not! Many contemporary manufactured limited editions become scarce after only a few years, and is not the artist "one-of-a-kind" creation potentially a rare piece?

ATTRIBUTES TO LOOK FOR IN AN OLD BEAR

If your reason for buying is just because you love looking after old bears, then probably all you will need to do is make eye contact (with the bear, not the vendor) and if you are not immediately attracted, then it is more than likely that you never will be!

First, character, which is a very subjective matter, is probably the essential factor. Condition will also be an important consideration in old bears. This is a matter of personal preference as to what you are prepared to accept. One should not expect bears to be in pristine condition; indeed well-loved bears are frequently far better characters when they have been played with.

FAKES

It is sad to reflect that with greater public awareness of the potential value of an old teddy, unscrupulous people have now taken to faking bears. If you accept that manufacturers make pretty good copies of their old bears, and that some artists are capable of producing really good old-looking bears, then you realize how easy it is to mislead the inexperienced collector. Faking can therefore be a very lucrative pastime for crooks!

Most people involved in faking bears are fairly unsophisticated, so they frequently let themselves down, though occasionally you just might come up against a good forgery, so be careful – and remember it is not necessarily the most expensive bear that can provide the forger with a good living! If you are in the slightest doubt or suspicious, leave the bear well alone!

SPECIALIST COLLECTORS' SHOPS

In the USA, UK and the Netherlands specialist collectors' shops are plentiful and they are now beginning to spring up in other countries too. It is necessary to define what a specialist collectors' shop constitutes. In our view it is a shop that caters exclusively to the collector and not tourist or off-the-street trade, and certainly not a gift, antique or general toy shop. While many of the latter may be perfectly reliable, they cannot ever be considered in the same category as the specialist shop which has dedicated itself totally to serving collectors. Some specialist shops deal only in old bears, while others sell contemporary and artist collectibles, and some deal in all three categories.

Collectors will soon discover which shops to patronize, and those which can be entirely relied upon for their professional ethical approach and standards. As with all collectibles, there are specialists who have been established much longer than others, are highly regarded with a reputation gained over the years for fair dealing. In general, these dealers are also capable of providing a reliable advisory service for valuation and identification.

ABOVE The button is missing, but the quality and design tell you this bear was made by Steiff (1907/08). It is less risky to buy bears like this from reputable dealers.

– CHECK POINTS FOR CONDITION –

Compare the colour of mohair in the joints with the rest of the bear as you can determine just how faded the bear actually is. It might be seriously faded but perhaps it has just grown old gracefully just like us humans. Mohair should generally be in satisfactory condition.

The facial embroidering should match the general demeanor of the bear but if it is bright and fresh, it was probably added recently. This would not perhaps matter too much but so often the wrong style of nose or mouth is sewn, giving the bear quite a false look. Of course this could have happened 40 years before on a visit to a teddy bear hospital, which is why you need to know as much as possible about the original style of nose.

Are the eyes original? There is a very good chance that they are not! If not, make sure they are the right size and colour and have been fitted properly.

Are the limbs well retained or have some discreetly hidden stitches been added to anchor the head or legs?

Are there any tears in the fabric, split seams, or damaged pads?

Does the voice box or squeaker work? Most of them do not and sadly the modern day replacement is often poor in comparison and distinctly noticeable.

– HOW TO SPOT A FAKE –

Rub your hands fairly lightly over the bear's fur – if your hands soil easily, it is likely that the grime was recently applied.

Smell the bear – it should have a natural old fusty smell and not a distinct odour of tobacco or dirt.

Look at the wear and tear. Cuts and tears are rarely a precise clean cut such as one made by a knife. Mohair wear is naturally intermittent and uneven. Therefore, look closely at the backing of the pile and any fine line marks caused by wire brush or sandpaper, frequently used to enhance wear, will be obvious. A disc or brush applied to an electric drill will leave a distinct circular pattern.

However well kept, most old bears of 40 or more years inevitably have suffered discoloration of some form or other. Look in the joints and you will see the bear's natural colour but expect some deterioration elsewhere. The fur of a recently made bear looks fairly consistent all over.

Finally, just hold the bear because modern filled bears look and feel distinctively different from old ones, although this will require some experience to recognize.

FURTHER INFORMATION & ADDRESSES

In order to derive the maximum benefit from collecting teddy bears, you owe it to yourself to obtain as much knowledge as is possible. The more proficient you are at identifying old bears, recognizing a good bargain, or appreciating investment potential, the less likely you are to make a serious – and therefore costly– mistake. The following sources may help to improve your knowledge.

MUSEUMS

These are just a few museums you should *not* miss:

USA

The Teddy Bear Museum of Naples, Florida

UK

The Cotswold Teddy Bear Museum, High Street, Broadway, Worcestershire WR12 7AJ
The Bear Museum, 38 Dragon Street, Petersfield, Hampshire GU31 4JJ

GERMANY

Margarete Steiff Museum, Allen Strasse 2, D-7928 Giengen (Brenz)

SHOWS AND CONVENTIONS

These can be both tremendous fun and beneficial in providing opportunities to add to your collection and share joyful experiences with other collectors.

USA

ABC Unlimited Promotions Shows, Schaumberg, Illinois, and other locations *(several)*
Bill Boyd's Teddy Bear Jubilee, Kansas City, Missouri *(annual)*
Serena Cohen's Liberty Artist Bear Show, Philadelphia Pennsylvania *(annual)*
Disneyland Doll and Bear Convention, Anaheim, California *(annual)*
Disney World Doll and Bear Conventions, Florida *(annual)*
Donna Harrison's Shows and Convention, Baltimore, Maryland *(twice yearly)*
ILTBC Convention, Orange, California *(annual)*
Linda Mullins Shows, San Diego, California *(twice yearly)*
Steve Schutt's Teddy Bear Reunion in the Heartland, Clarion, Iowa *(every five years, next in June 2000)*

JAPAN

Japan Teddy Bear Association Convention, Tokyo *(annual)*

BRITAIN

Margaret and Gerry Grey's Teddies of the World Convention, location to be confirmed *(every three years, next in 1996)*
Hugglets, Teddy Bear Fairs, and events, London and Stratford-on-Avon *(several)*
Teddy Bear Times, British Bear Festivals, Croydon, and Hove, East Sussex *(twice yearly)*

THE NETHERLANDS

Rob and Inge Kuiters, Bear Festival Amerongen Castle *(every May)*

MAGAZINES

There are many specialist magazines published throughout the world.
Bear Facts Review, published in Australia.
Beer Bericht, published in the Netherlands (four issues)
Ciesliks Teddy und seine Freunde, published in Germany
de Teddy-Beer, published in the Netherlands (four issues)
Hugglets Teddy Bear Magazine, published in UK (four issues)
Teddy Bear and Friends, published in USA (six issues)
Teddy Bear Review, published in USA (five issues)
Teddy Bear Times, published in UK (six issues)